DRUGS

WHAT YOUR KID
SHOULD KNOW

a parent handbook by
K. Wayne Hindmarsh, Ph.D., FCSFS

DRUGS
WHAT YOUR KID
SHOULD KNOW

by

K.Wayne Hindmarsh, Ph.D., FCSFS

Canadian Cataloguing in Publication Data

Hindmarsh, K. Wayne

Drugs : What Your Kid Should Know

3rd ed. —

Includes bibliographical references.
ISBN 0–9695996–1–7

1. Substance abuse. 2. Youth – Substance abuse.
I. Title.

HV5801.H55   1992   362.29′0835   C92–098048–1

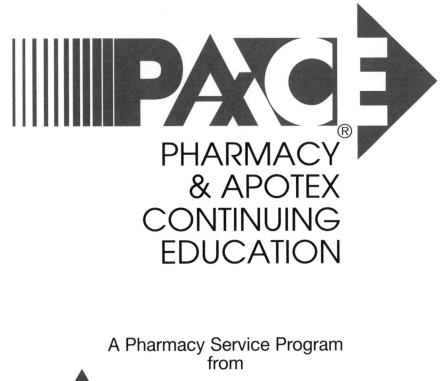

PHARMACY
& APOTEX
CONTINUING
EDUCATION

A Pharmacy Service Program
from

Λ portion of the proceeds from the sale of this book will be donated
to educational programs relating to drug and substance abuse.

"As partners with the pharmacy profession in the healthcare system,
it is fundamental to the Apotex corporate philosophy to support
through educational grants, projects of this kind."

To: Lois, Carla and Ryan
Your constant support has provided me
with the desire to help others.
Thank you for your love and continual encouragement.

PREFACE

Drug use/abuse continues to be one of our major social problems. Use of legal (tobacco and alcohol) and illegal drugs has increased since the early 1990s. Drug use is a burden to our health care budgets, to the individuals involved in the drug taking, and to their families and friends. There are a number of pro-drug lobbyists who would have us believe we are infringing on an individual's personal rights if we take a 'no-nonsense' stand.

This book was written to provide parents and youth with scientific information related to the health effects of the most commonly abused drugs. Why another book on drug abuse? It is true there are many sources of drug information but often they are unavailable in either a comprehensive format or in any one single source. Other books are written for health professionals and may be difficult to comprehend. This book will hopefully aid in filling the gap, providing a resource that is both comprehensive and easy to understand. Since the first issue of this book was written, the Internet has become a very useful source of information; however, it must be viewed cautiously to ensure the information retrieved is based on sound, substantive evidence. Some useful Internet sites have been included in this revision.

This revised edition also contains a number of other new additions. Chapters describing the health effects of the use of tobacco, Ecstasy, and party drugs (Rohypnol, GHB, ketamine and others) have been added. Other chapters have simply been updated, where appropriate. The book begins with an overview of drug use in the new millennium, and provides information related to prevalence of use, costs to society, and harm reduction, as well as views of respected scientists and groups working in the drug use area. At the end of each chapter is a set of questions that may be used to focus on your understanding of what was just read.

The author has taken care to provide accurate information based on personal experiences during his work in forensic science and from the scientific literature. A reference list has been included. Any references inadvertently omitted will be included in the next printing. It is not the intent of the author to claim this information as his own, but rather to acknowledge it was retrieved from many sources. The case studies, in most instances, are from the medical literature. The persons referred to in the cases are fictitious. Any similarity to known drug users is purely coincidental.

It is well known that an informed parent is best equipped to prevent children from becoming involved with drugs. This resource will provide parents, youth and other consumers with up-to-date, factual information for the most commonly abused drugs. After reading this handbook, parents and youth should have a better understanding of the drugs they may encounter. The information contained within these pages will hopefully lead to meaningful dialogues. Without a doubt, parents who talk to their children about drugs in an informed manner will see positive results.

K. Wayne Hindmarsh, Ph.D., FCSFS
Faculty of Pharmacy
University of Toronto
Toronto, Canada

ACKNOWLEDGEMENTS

This handbook was made possible through the support and direction from many dedicated friends, family and colleagues. I wish to express my sincere appreciation to them all.

The drawings, interspersed throughout this handbook, were done by Ms. May Chow, B.S.P., a graduate of the College of Pharmacy, University of Saskatchewan. Ms. Chow is a pharmacist in Regina, Saskatchewan (Canada) and is the mother of two children. Thank you, May, for your excellent contribution. Your drawings make the reading so much more interesting and superbly visualize some of the hazardous effects of drug use.

I particularly wish to thank those who provided meaningful input during the first draft of this handbook. Their valuable suggestions carried through to this edition. These people include: my wife, Lois Hindmarsh, Dorothy Smith, Yvonne Shevchuk, Larry Korchinski, Ken Ready, Eloise Opheim, Richard Muenz and Shelly Porter-Serviss.

A special thank you to the Department of Professional Affairs at Apotex Inc., in particular, its director, Alan Kyte, for encouraging this recent revision, and to Matthew Lee and Allan Malek for making this handbook available as a resource to pharmacists throughout Canada.

K.W.H.

CONTENTS

DRUG USE IN THE NEW MILLENNIUM

DRUG USE IN THE NEW MILLENNIUM

As we enter a new millennium, it is useful to begin by reflecting on the magnitude of drug use/abuse. A number of reports have shown an upward trend in use from that seen in the early 1990s. The Centre for Addiction and Mental Health in Canada (Ontario) found that after a lengthy period of decline during the 1980s, there was a resurgence in the 1990s, most notably in the use of alcohol, heavy drinking episodes, cigarettes, cannabis (marijuana), MDMA (Ecstasy), PCP, hallucinogens and cocaine. In Western Canada, the Parent Resources Institute for Drug Education (PRIDE Canada) also saw increases in use during the late 1990s. A dramatic increase in marijuana use among senior high school students (more than one-third of these students) was noted. Not surprisingly, marijuana use increased along with cigarette use. Significantly higher uses of cocaine and hallucinogens from those seen in the early 1990s (usage increased threefold) were also reported.

While drug use declined slightly in 1997 and 1998 in the United States, an August 1997 report by the National Center on Addiction and Substance Abuse stated, "if drug use among teenagers continues at current rates or even if such use is slightly reduced, America will enter the new millennium with more teenagers using drugs, since the number of adolescents is rising and continues to rise through the early years of the next century." The National Institute on Drug Abuse (United States) saw no significant changes in 1999 in the use of marijuana, amphetamines, hallucinogens, tranquilizers, or heroin but noted that there were significant changes in the use of other drugs. There was a reduction in the use of crack cocaine by 8th- and 10th-graders following several years of gradually increasing use, a reduction in the use of crystal methamphetamine, or 'Ice', among 12th-graders, a reduction in cigarette smoking among 8th-graders, but an increase in the use of MDMA among 10th- and 12th-graders, and an increase in the use of anabolic steroids among 8th- and 10th-graders, primarily among boys.

Another interesting finding was reported in January 2000 by the National Center on Addiction and Substance Abuse. They found that smoking, drinking and drug use among young teens is higher in rural America than in the nation's large urban centers. Eighth- graders living in rural America are more likely to smoke marijuana, use crack cocaine, drink alcohol, get drunk and smoke cigarettes. Tenth-grader drug use exceeds urban use for every drug, except MDMA and marijuana. Twelfth-grader use exceeds their urban counterparts for cocaine, crack, amphetamines, inhalants, alcohol, cigarettes and smokeless tobacco.

While one-quarter of students reports using no drugs (including alcohol and tobacco), approximately one-quarter use alcohol and tobacco products and over one-third use illicit drugs. It is evident that drug use in North America is still prevalent and is a concern, since the youth are the future of our country!

The Financial Implications of Substance Use

According to Drug Watch International, substance abuse is the number one health problem in America. More deaths, illness and disabilities derive from substance abuse than from any other preventable health condition. The financial costs, according to the Center on Addiction and Substance Abuse at Columbia University, approach $400 billion annually. This figure does not include all the personal life tragedies incurred by the addicted individuals and the suffering borne by their families, children and friends. If costs for alcohol and tobacco use are excluded, the illegal drug costs in the United States are estimated to be approximately $110 billion each year. In Canada, a report provided by the Canadian Centre on Substance Abuse estimates the costs to be $18.45 billion per year or 2.7% of the Gross Domestic Product (GDP). This figure represents the most optimistic estimate. However, the Canadian report further states, *"the actual number is probably higher and could be significantly higher."* Consider the estimated direct health care costs of substance use for each of the Canadian provinces (1992 data): British Columbia ($487 million), Alberta ($350 million), Saskatchewan ($119 million), Manitoba ($161 million), Ontario ($1.5 billion), Quebec ($1 billion), New Brunswick ($100 million), Nova Scotia ($146 million), Prince Edward Island ($17 million) and Newfoundland ($71 million). It is interesting to dream of all the many other things the government could do with this money.

Drug habits are expensive!

While we are concerned with illegal drugs and their effects on our adolescents, one should not forget the fact that the major costs of substance abuse are associated with two legal drugs – tobacco and alcohol. In 1992, there were 40,930 deaths in Canada attributable to substance abuse. Tobacco accounted for 33,498 of these deaths, alcohol 6,701 and illicit drugs 732. This represents 21% of the total mortality for that year – a significant percentage! One might assume that this mortality rate has not decreased in 2000, since drug use has substantially increased since the early 1990s.

How Can Parents Help?

Criminal justice, transportation, and emergency-room studies conclude overwhelmingly that violent episodes, accidents, crime, and other anti-social behaviours among adolescents are often drug related. In the face of widespread drug use among children, Drug Watch International believes that preventing drug use should be the goal of every parent. Parents need to become informed not only about which drugs our children are using but also with the agenda and strategies of those who would legitimize, legalize, and sell drugs to our children. Well-informed parents can successfully stand against drug use and vigorously counter 'pro-drug' propaganda with facts and caring intervention in the lives of youth. In a survey of nearly 200,000 students, drug use declined sharply among students whose parents frequently discussed drugs with them. As an example, marijuana use dropped by 29% among high school students whose parents talked about drugs 'a lot'.

Understanding the harmful effects of abused substances is a vital part of a prevention strategy with respect to alcohol, tobacco and other drugs. Education must be presented with a clear 'no-use' message and discussed at a level that matches the age and capabilities of our children.

Harm Reduction

The term 'harm reduction' is consistently being bantered about. While this term is difficult to criticize given its converse position, which would be to 'increase harm', the context of its use needs to be seriously considered. There are two types of harm reduction. One is a genuine compassion for the addicted individual and employs harm reduction strategies as part of a treatment program, with the ultimate goal to rid the person of drug dependency. An example of this type of harm reduction is providing methadone for the treatment of narcotic abuse. The second type of harm reduction is a movement that supports the liberalization of drug laws and/or legalization of the drugs themselves. This concept accepts a level of, and inherently promotes, drug use. It is a theory promoted by pro-drug advocates which holds that society must accept levels of use of the drugs and teach 'responsible use' to reduce the harm.

A statement by Dr. Robert Gilkeson, a noted child and adolescent neuropsychiatrist, clearly addresses the issues of harm reduction. "The toxic properties of chemical molecules and their cellular damage are not matters of opinion or debate. They are not determined by adolescent servicemen, or by scientifically uneducated lawyers, legislators, judges, or doctors without the facts. We cannot vote for or against the 'toxicity' of a drug. How much a drug impairs cell structure or chemical function is neither subject to nor governed by congressional committee, public referendum, or the federal constitution. Everyone is entitled to his own 'opinion'. He is not entitled to his own 'facts'. Chemically, marijuana is a far more dangerous drug than most of the scientifically ignorant media and American consumer have been duped into believing."

Drug Watch International, in their 2000 edition of position statements, provides the following opinion. "Drug users, like any other members of society, must be accountable for their actions. Every segment of society must send the message that drug use and drug use behaviour is not tolerated. Drug user accountability must be a cornerstone of national and international policy." It is interesting to look at the initiatives taken by various world governments and to compare their standards with that of North America. "In Sweden, drug prevention measures have high priority within the police, the customs service, the public prosecution service, the prison and probation service, social services, schools and various leisure activities. Experimental use of cannabis and other drugs is very low in this country, and for many years drug use among young people has been very limited. Their aim is to have drug abuse remain a socially unaccepted form of behaviour." How does Sweden's philosophy compare with those of Canada and the United States? In Canada, the most successful strategy to date consisted of three initiatives – enforcement, prevention and treatment. Using this formula, a downward trend of drug use among the student population was enjoyed until approximately 1992/1993, when the trend reversed and drug use began to climb. Analysis of this shift revealed that the topic of substance abuse had dropped off the political agendas of all levels of government, and few resources were dedicated to it. Presently, in Canada, there is an organized campaign to redirect the resources from strategies designed to eliminate inappropriate drug use to those directed at the symptoms of drug use. These strategies come under the umbrella of harm reduction. In the United States, throughout the 1970s, marijuana was decriminalized in 11 states, drug addicts were viewed as victims, and cocaine decriminalization was proposed. The largest increase in youth using drugs in the history of the United States followed this permissive attitude. Crime and drug-related social problems threatened the health and well-being of citizens. In the early 1980s, the public and law enforcement applied pressure to hold drug users accountable for their illegal drug use. Drug use was reduced by over 50%. Following this success, drug legalization advocates initiated a sophisticated public relations campaign aimed at weakening the public's aversion toward illegal drug use, citing it as an infringement of personal rights. In the early 1990s, the battle against drugs began to lose national focus, and thus momentum. Anti-drug messages and social attitudes started to soften, the media and music began to 'reglamorize' drug use, and among school children, drug use began to climb (teen marijuana usage doubling over a three-year span) after a 12-year decline.

Summary

It is evident that drug/substance use is still a major issue as we enter the new millennium. There are many conflicting views as to how we should deal with the issue. One must form educated opinions and discuss these with our children. They are our 'prized possessions' and the next generation of leaders of our great nation. For additional information see p.167 on "Signs and Symptoms of Drug Use."

TOBACCO

WHY YOU SHOULD 'BUTT' OUT

TOBACCO

Why You Should 'Butt' Out

Tobacco use is the leading preventable cause of premature death. It is estimated that tobacco causes more than 400,000 deaths in the United States each year – a figure that represents 20% of all deaths. This high percentage is believed to be similar for all of the developed countries, including Canada. In fact, smoking kills more people each year than AIDS, alcohol, auto accidents, homicide, illegal drugs, fires and suicides combined (according to Smokefree Education Services Inc., New York).

The Secretary of the U.S. Department of Health and Human Services, Dr. Donna Shalala, has been quoted as saying, "today nearly 3,000 young people across the United States will begin smoking regularly. Of these 3,000 young people, 1,000 will lose that gamble to diseases caused by smoking. The net effect of this is that among young children living in America today, 5 million will die an early, preventable death because of a decision made as a child." Since the first Surgeon General's report on smoking and health in 1964, our knowledge of the health consequences of tobacco use has increased phenomenally. It is now well documented that smoking can cause chronic lung disease, coronary heart disease and stroke, as well as cancers of the lungs, larynx, esophagus, mouth and bladder. In addition, smoking is known to contribute to cancers of the cervix, pancreas and kidneys. Researchers have identified more than 40 chemicals in tobacco smoke that cause cancer. Smokeless tobacco and cigars also have deadly consequences, including lung, laryngeal, esophageal and oral cancers. In 1930, the lung cancer death rate for men was 4.9 per 100,000; in 1990, the rate increased to 75.6 per 100,000 (an increase of over 1500%). The costs to society are enormous – $100 billion each year in the United States and between $7.8 and $11.1 billion in Canada.

Is it any wonder that cigarettes are implicated in causing so many health problems? One report referred to the chemicals in tobacco smoke as "a lethal cocktail – a horrifying list of toxic chemicals". There are '600 poisons in every cigarette'. The British government published a list of the ingredients found in a cigarette and on this list were such things as "a paint stripper, a toilet cleaner, a lighter fuel, the chemicals of mothballs, a poison used in gas chambers, a rocket fuel, and many other chemicals." A complete list of the chemicals may be obtained through the Action on Smoking and Health (ASH) website – www.http://ash.org.

Prevalence of Smoking

Cigarette use has increased and remains at a significant level. Canadian and American studies show that between 29% and 55% of students smoked at least once in the year. Junior high student (grades 6 to 8) use is also shockingly high (37.5%), although this varies from community to community.

Modes of Tobacco Use

Most tobacco users smoke **cigarettes** and get the desired effects by inhaling the smoke into the lungs. A smaller number smoke cigars and pipes. **Cigar smokers** often do not inhale the smoke since the nicotine levels are sufficiently high to be absorbed through the mouth. In a 1996 U.S. study, 26.7% of the high school students smoked at least one cigar during the year (this translates to 4.3 million males and 1.7 million females between the ages of 14 and 19 years). More surprisingly, between 13% and 15% of grade 9 students in two areas of New York smoked a cigar during the month prior to a study conducted in their schools. Cigar smoking has been implicated in cancers of the mouth, larynx, esophagus and lung, and as a contributing cause of chronic obstructive pulmonary disease. Despite these risks, total cigar consumption in the United States was 4.5 billion in 1996 and the use of larger cigars increased by a whopping 44.5% between 1993 and 1996.

While not all **pipe smokers** inhale (since the nicotine level is high and may be absorbed through the mouth), those that do tend to inhale more vigorously than cigarette smokers. This results in more nicotine being absorbed. Another concern with pipe smoking is the smoldering tobacco in the pipe bowl, which has the same effect as inhaling sidestream smoke from cigarettes (see next page).

Cigarette manufacturing has undergone a number of changes. Most smokers were smoking unfiltered cigarettes in the early 1950s when cigarettes were first implicated as causing lung cancer. A filter was subsequently designed to reduce the tar inhaled and low tar cigarettes were produced. However, this change has not decreased the possibility of getting cancer since smokers compensate for the changes in the product by smoking more vigorously (inhaling more often and more deeply), and by blocking the filter's ventilation holes. They also tend to smoke more cigarettes than normal.

Hand-rolled cigarettes from India, called 'bidis' (pronounced 'beedees'), have become an increasingly popular alternative to conventional cigarettes with teens in the United States. However, they are not less addicting and have been found to contain higher nicotine concentrations than unfiltered cigarettes (as much as 28% more nicotine). Bidis are sold in tobacco shops and other outlets in colourful packages with flavour choices such as cinnamon, orange and chocolate.

Few individuals receive their tobacco high from 'smokeless tobacco'. Smokeless tobacco includes such products as snuff or chewing tobacco. Tobacco chewing is common among some athletes, who claim it keeps their mouths from going dry. Because the use of smokeless tobacco causes cancers of the mouth and neck, it has been banned by many high school and university athletic associations.

Often we forget that there is an involuntary method of using tobacco. This method is often referred to as 'passive smoking'. The sidestream smoke from a smoldering cigarette, cigar or pipe does not pass through a filter or through the lungs of the smoker and is extremely potent, containing more tar, nicotine, gases and other particles than the smoke inhaled by the smoker. Sidestream smoke is dangerous and may cause allergic reactions, respiratory diseases and even lung cancer. Children of parents who smoke have increased incidence of respiratory disease compared to children of non-smoking parents. They also have more chronic ear infections, frequent coughs and more phlegm. A study in the United States found that when a non-smoker married a smoker there was a twofold-increased risk of lung cancer. Another investigation revealed the risk for coronary heart disease for lifelong non-smoking men whose wives smoked, compared with that of men whose wives did not smoke, was more than doubled. This evidence is surely a legitimate reason for demanding a smoke-free environment. It is your right and no one should be afraid to demand it!

Effects of Tobacco Use

It is hard to believe that, in the 1600s, tobacco was likened to penicillin. A London physician suggested using tobacco in the following manner:

> *"to cure deafness, a drop of the juice in the ear; to cure headache, a green tobacco leaf on the head; for redness of the face, apply the juice or the ointment of tobacco leaf; for a toothache, tie a tobacco leaf over the aching region; for cough, boil the leaves and shake the syrup on the stomach; for stomach pain and to take away the crudities of young and old, apply hot tobacco over the region of the belly and re-heat whenever they got cool."*

Tobacco was recommended for treatment of burns, wounds, warts, corns, cancers, worms, stomach pain, and diseases of the liver, spleen and uterus. Fortunately, by the end of the 17th century, these claims were not substantiated.

A stimulating effect occurs with smoking or chewing tobacco, resulting in a pleasurable sensation, not unlike a 'high'. Users may find the effect relaxing but it also can be stressful due to chemicals released in the body from tobacco products. Nicotine is an addictive substance. It causes the heart to beat more rapidly and results in the veins and arteries constricting, thus requiring the heart to work harder – raising blood pressure. It also stimulates the central nervous system.

Nicotine has complex and unpredictable actions on the body. In tobacco smoke, suspended on very small particles of tar, nicotine is absorbed into the bloodstream with the same speed as an injection. It reaches the brain within 8 seconds after inhalation, giving what is described as a 'rush'. This is why the craving for tobacco is quickly satisfied. Nicotine is linked to a number of problems, ranging from heart disease to lung cancer. While the cancer may not be due to nicotine itself, the nicotine, when smoked, is converted to a nitrosated product that is a cancer-causing substance. One report suggests that smoking will reduce your life expectancy by 5 to 8 years, or approximately 5.5 minutes for every cigarette smoked. Nicotine is only one of the toxic components in tobacco. There are at least 4,000 other harmful substances in the deadly smoke.

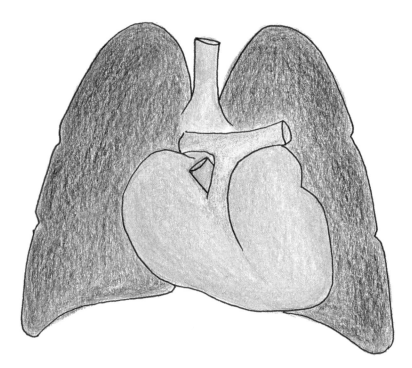

"Dirty Lungs"

Carbon monoxide is another of the toxic chemicals in the smoke of tobacco products. This poisonous gas has a profound effect on red blood cells. Carbon monoxide combines with red blood cells at a faster rate than oxygen. This leads to the formation of carboxyhemoglobin, a substance incapable of carrying oxygen. The end result is that there is less oxygen transported to our most important organs, the brain and the heart. The heart works harder and develops a thickening of the walls resulting in possible heart failure. The carbon monoxide may also play a role in the facial wrinkling effects of tobacco use (which was noted as early as 1856 but not established as an effect of smoking until the 1970s). The skin of smokers can be pale and yellowish with some of the following features:

> *facial wrinkles found around the upper and lower lips and around the eyes; a gaunt look, with bony facial appearance; slightly pigmented, grey appearance to the skin; slightly orange, purple, and red complexion.*

Why would any young person want to hasten this rather unpleasant facial appearance? The aging process might do the same but certainly not as quickly.

The U.S. Department of Health and Human Services, in their 1994 report from the Centers for Disease Control and Prevention, summarizes the health consequences of tobacco use among young people as follows: "Active smoking by young people is associated with significant health problems during childhood and adolescence and with increased risk factors for health problems in adulthood. Cigarette smoking during adolescence appears to reduce the rate of lung growth and the level of maximum lung function that can be achieved." Young smokers are likely to be less physically fit than young nonsmokers; fitness levels are inversely related to the duration and intensity of smoking. Adolescent smokers are more likely than their non-smoking peers to experience shortness of breath, coughing spells, phlegm production, wheezing, and overall diminished physical health. Smoking poses a clear risk for respiratory symptoms and problems that are risk factors for other chronic conditions in adulthood, including chronic obstructive pulmonary disease.

Cardiovascular disease is the leading cause of death among adults. Atherosclerosis may begin in childhood and become clinically significant by young adulthood. Cigarette smoking has been shown to be a primary risk factor for coronary heart disease, arteriosclerotic peripheral vascular disease and stroke. Smoking by children and adolescents is associated with an increased risk of early atherosclerotic lesions and increased risk for cardiovascular disease. These risk factors include increased levels of the 'bad' low-density lipoprotein (LDL) cholesterol, increased triglycerides, and reduced levels of 'good' high-density lipoproteins (HDL).

Smokeless tobacco use is associated with effects ranging from halitosis (bad breath) to various forms of oral cancer. Periodontal degeneration, soft tissue lesions, and general systematic alterations are also reported with its use.

The health effects of tobacco use may be summarized simply as follows:

> Mouth, lung, throat, larynx, esophagus, stomach, pancreas, uterus, cervix, kidney and bladder cancers (pipe smoking has been implicated in lip cancer just as cigar smoking causes mouth cancer); some types of leukemia.
>
> Heart attacks, heart failure and strokes.
>
> Lung problems.
>
> Serious problems during pregnancy, including miscarriage, premature birth, birth defects, developmental problems and low birth weight. Additionally, nicotine depresses appetite and smoking reduces the ability to carry oxygen; the fetus is thus deprived of nourishment and oxygen.

Smokers continually experience nicotine withdrawal. Drawing smoke into the lung satisfies this withdrawal. Withdrawal symptoms include changes in heart rate, blood pressure, appetite, temperature and digestion. It can also produce other unpleasant effects such as anxiety, difficulty in sleeping, nausea, irritability and a 'tired feeling'. It is very hard to quit smoking. Many adolescent smokers would like to quit and have tried unsuccessfully on a number of occasions.

King James I of England, in 1604, described smoking as:

> *"a custom loathsome to the Eye, hateful to the Nose, harmful to the Brain, dangerous to the Lungs, and the black stinking fumes thereof, resembling the horrible Stigian smoke of the pit that is bottomless."*

He declared tobacco to be immoral and unhealthy. Death penalties were imposed upon smokers in Russia, Turkey, Persia and even in parts of India, where the Emperor ordered smokers to be punished by slitting their lips.

Effects of Advertising

Tobacco companies spend $15.5 million **daily** on marketing their products. Much of it is an attempt to attract children. It is a fact that 9 out of 10 adults hooked on cigarettes started as kids. Without our children, tobacco companies have no future. At the beginning of this chapter, we indicated that each day, 3,000 kids get hooked on tobacco. One in three will die from its use. The best way to prevent these early deaths is to stop smoking and do whatever possible to eliminate tobacco marketing that hooks kids. After all, if it were not effective, why would they spend the millions of dollars on advertising?

Efforts to prevent the use of tobacco products among our young people are crucial. Very few people begin to use tobacco as an adult; most begin before they leave high school. While we would not like to see the Emperor's punishment of slitting lips reinstated, it is time we seriously consider the health consequences and costs of tobacco use, the addicting potential and the effects on non-smokers who are inhaling sidestream smoke. Savings to the health care budgets and the benefits of a healthy lifestyle would be substantial if people would just 'butt out'.

LET'S SEE WHAT YOU'VE LEARNED ABOUT TOBACCO

Tobacco has been likened to the drug penicillin. Is this a good comparison?

What do you understand by the terms:

– Passive smoking?

– Smokeless tobacco?

– A lethal cocktail?

What effects does tobacco use have on the heart and brain?

What other effects could tobacco use have on you?

ALCOHOL

THE SIMPLE DRUG?

ALCOHOL
The Simple Drug?

How many times have you heard someone say after a wild party, "thank goodness they were only drinking alcohol" or "it's too bad but they're going to drink anyway and so it's not really a surprise"? This message seems to imply that alcohol is not as bad as other drugs. Alcohol is only a 'simple drug' from a chemical point of view.   Its molecular formula is simple and easy to remember (CH_3CH_2OH). It is, however, safe to assume that if this simple drug was discovered today it probably would not be legalized.   Alcohol has ruined lives, caused deaths and is responsible for millions of dollars in health care expenditure. Education has had a considerable effect in informing the public as to the consequences of using, and in particular, abusing this so-called simple drug but there is still more to be done. Statistics continue to show alcohol as the **number one** drug of abuse among youth. Yes, alcohol **is** a drug, just like heroin, marijuana, cocaine, or prescription drugs.

The following true cases are illustrative of problems associated with alcohol abuse.

> *Barbara, a 12-year-old girl, was admitted to the hospital with a three-hour history of vomiting after which she passed out. Upon arrival at the hospital she appeared drowsy but responded to the questions of the doctor. She denied use of alcohol or other drugs and no alcohol was detected on her breath. However, laboratory results confirmed a blood alcohol concentration of 0.21%, i.e. in each 100 ml of blood there was 210 milligrams of alcohol. In other words, this represents a Breathalyzer reading of 0.21 (legal limit in Canada, 0.08). Only then, did Barbara admit to drinking gin and tonic with her friends.*

Brian, a 10-year-old boy, was heard calling from the bathroom one night. His father, responding quickly to his cries, found his son drowsy, confused and frothing at the mouth. After some time, Brian's condition worsened to the point of vomiting. He was quickly transported to the hospital. Although he was quite drowsy when he arrived, he was able to respond to commands. When questioned about the possibility of alcohol or drug ingestion, both were denied. However, a laboratory determination revealed an alcohol level of 0.11%.

Brad, a 17-year-old teenager, had been drinking heavily over a four-month period. He apparently consumed large quantities of beer (up to 5 litres) and wine daily. Suddenly he decided to discontinue his abusive habit and within 10 days began to experience bizarre behaviour (eye blinking and rolling, neck snapping, facial contortions, shoulder shrugging), and became very talkative. On medical examination it appeared these signs were due to alcohol withdrawal (a term used to describe the symptoms seen on sudden stoppage of drinking alcohol). Many of the signs disappeared within one month; however, he continued to experience occasional eye blinking and shoulder shrugging for some time.

Alcohol in Perspective

A number of groups have conducted drug prevalence surveys in an attempt to follow trends in alcohol use. A study conducted in 1999, by the Centre for Addiction and Mental Health in Ontario, Canada, revealed that the continuing upswing in drug use among Ontario youth seen since 1993 has been moving upwards to the point where the current rates of use do not differ appreciably from the late 1970s. The percentage of students who drink alcohol rose significantly from 56.5% to 65.7% in 1993. More students reported weekly drinking and drinkers reported more episodes of heavy drinking (consumption of five or more drinks on a single occasion). So what? The fact is these students, for the most part, are *under the legal drinking age!* Drinking alcohol one to

Adult lack of concern.

seven times a week is considered heavy use. In other words, it is not just the occasional drink. Thirty percent of grade 12 students reported heavy use of beer and 20.0% reported heavy use of liquor. Ten percent of the grade 9 students reported heavy use of beer and 7.5% reported heavy liquor use. It may be argued that drinking once a week is hardly considered heavy use but keep in mind the fact that young people generally drink to get a 'buzz'. Each drinking episode is more than just one bottle or can of the foaming liquid. A significant increase in the reported heavy consumption of alcohol between eighth and ninth grades was also noted in the above study. In some parts of Canada, ninth grade is the first exposure to high school and the 'big boys'!

The legal drinking age varies from country to country and also within countries. For example, the legal drinking age in the United States is 21 while in Canada some provinces have set the legal age at 18 years and others at 19. Why is there a legal drinking age? The reasons are often forgotten. It's not to create jobs for the police and court personnel. To put it simply, young people often cannot handle alcohol. Alcohol profoundly affects the structure and function of the central nervous system, particularly at the level of the neuronal membrane (development of the nervous system), where the effects are quite selective. In fact, the U.S. Department of Health and Human Services, in their sixth special report to the U.S. Congress on Alcohol and Health (1987), suggests that one of the principal aims of alcohol-related research on the brain is to correlate the changes in the neurochemistry and anatomy with behavioural and physiological responses to alcohol. They further state that the memory system of the brain is disrupted during alcohol intoxication. Although there is no proof that moderate alcohol consumption will cause permanent structural brain damage, some evidence suggests that moderate social drinking may compromise cognitive efficiency (the process of knowing, including awareness and judgement). This could partially explain the reason physicians are seeing patients, in their late twenties, who are no more mature than 18-year-olds. The heavy use of alcohol during their teen years could have slowed their brain development. Remember that growing tissues are more prone to the toxic effects of drugs, including alcohol, than are mature tissues. For this reason, young people can become 'full-blown alcoholics' much quicker than adults.

Some provinces in Canada tried lowering the drinking age with the hope that if it were legal to drink, less alcohol would be consumed. In other words, there would not be the same challenge or thrill of trying something illegal. The experiment failed! Alcohol consumption and the problems associated with its use increased. Unfortunately, the beverage chosen by youth is not just beer (**'just beer'** is terminology that should not be used since one beer has just as much alcohol as one shot of liquor – that is, beer can also produce the same effects as liquor and wine).

Are adults to blame for the excessive use of alcohol by youth? If they do not provide clear-cut reasons for not drinking, the answer is 'yes'. Young people look up to adults and parents for guidance. Even though they may not always agree with the guidelines imposed, parents who do take a stand are to be respected. Adults who do not agree with the drinking age imposed by their government should insist on an open forum. The debate would be interesting. The legal drinking age could rise!

Short-Term Effects of Alcohol

Alcohol is consumed primarily for its euphoric (feeling of well-being or elation) and intoxicating effects. As a result, there is the misconception that alcohol is a stimulant. In fact, alcohol has just the opposite effect and is actually a depressant – depressing brain function. While some people may become more sociable, others turn moody and obnoxious. The latter effects are often not perceived by the drinking person. As alcohol intake continues during a drinking bout, more of the brain is affected. Continued intake depresses more of the brain and, if enough is ingested, can lead to sleep and more seriously, death.

Any alcohol consumption will effect judgement and self-control. These functions are impaired long before physical incoordination is apparent. People might not realize the problem and may misjudge the ability of their friends to drive. The truth is, any alcohol ingestion may be too much for some to safely drive a motor vehicle. This is particularly true for young people. The effects of alcohol on their judgement are more pronounced. A young person likes to experience a 'buzz'. A 'buzz' goes along with a good time. Driving a vehicle definitely should not be attempted at this stage.

A number of programs have been developed to cut down on the number of motor vehicle accidents. SADD (Students Against Driving Drunk) is a good example. Another one is the Designated Driver program, which has gained some popularity. Anything that can be done to prevent one of the major effects of alcohol in teens (death or disabling damage, such as quadriplegia or permanent paralysis) is worthwhile *but*

Sociability

the attitude that young people *will* drink has to be addressed! Why do we allow it? Young people should grow up drug-free, not with the attitude that a designated driver is the norm. Youth groups are multiplying across North America, which support the 'drug-free' concept. Adults should do all they can to support them. It's time to dispel the beliefs that nothing will work. If our children do not get the support from adults, alcohol problems will continue to escalate.

Television portrays 'good times' associated with drinking. Unfortunately, this is not the case, as many will verify. Accidents and violence are serious problems. Fights, break-ins and other crimes are the result of an altered reasoning ability caused by alcohol. Some rape victims were unable to defend themselves because they were under the influence of alcohol at the time of attack. Too often we excuse people for what they have done because they were 'under the influence' at the time – does this make sense?

Alcohol Effects on The Body

Alcohol acts on a system of nerve cells known as the 'reticular formation', which is located in the brain stem. When stimuli such as sound and pain are received, information is sent to the brain in the form of coded electrical impulses. This prompts the brain to identify the information and match it with memory. This identification initiates a response. Alcohol, even in small doses, suppresses this matching process. Individuals become less attentive and are preoccupied with their inner thoughts and emotions and a response may not be initiated or, if initiated, the response or reaction time is slowed.

The liver is an important organ. Humans cannot survive without it. Any substance taken orally passes though the liver before it reaches the blood stream. Substances are 'screened' by the liver and are seen as being something useful for the body, something that could be useful if converted into some other chemical structure, or something that should be gotten rid of. In order for a drug to be eliminated from the body, the liver will convert it to something that is easily excreted, either in the urine or faeces. Alcohol is eliminated primarily by chemical structural changes occurring in the liver, eventually being converted into carbon dioxide and water. It is eliminated at a constant rate, that is, blood alcohol concentrations decrease by a constant amount every hour. Blood alcohol concentrations decrease, on average, by 0.015% per hour after drinking has ceased. The elimination of alcohol from

26

blood cannot be speeded up by taking a cold shower, drinking black coffee or by any other means your friends might suggest. If sufficient alcohol is ingested during an 'evening out' with friends, it is possible the person is still legally drunk the next morning. The alcohol would not have been completely eliminated from the body and the blood level, the next morning, would still be above the legal limit of 0.05% or 0.08%. Adults should also keep this fact in mind when getting behind the wheel of an automobile the morning after 'a night on the town'.

Long-Term (Chronic) Effects of Alcohol

Some of the long-term effects of alcohol, seen after drinking alcohol for months or years, may also be seen after only short-term use (weeks or months). Therefore, don't think the following problems will not occur with just the occasional use of alcohol.

- Effects of Alcohol on the Gastrointestinal Tract (The Stomach and Intestine)

When food is eaten, it has to be broken down and digested. Alcohol is absorbed directly, without being broken down, through the walls of the stomach and the small intestines. Approximately 20% to 30% is absorbed through the stomach and the remainder through the small intestine. Once alcohol has moved into the blood, it is distributed throughout the body depending on water content. The brain has considerable water. Alcohol irritates the lining of the stomach and intestine causing a breakdown of the protective lining (mucosa). If this begins to happen, a noticeable effect might be heartburn or serious pain. The seriousness of this effect increases with increased amounts of alcohol consumed and with the increasing concentration of alcohol in the drink. If drinking continues, bleeding, ulcers and perforation (hole) of the stomach may result. Loss of blood, if excessive, is serious.

- Effects of Alcohol on the Liver

Liver cirrhosis (inflammation) cases are, for the most part, a result of heavy alcohol use. Alcohol and its breakdown products (metabolites) are toxic (poisonous) to the liver. Heavy consumption is often used as a substitute for food. The lack of food results in decreased nutrient and vitamin intake which can seriously effect the liver's normal functioning. For example, vitamin K, a necessary substance for the clotting process of blood, cannot be utilized and the alcoholic is thus known as a 'potential bleeder'. Furthermore, the damaged liver is unable to utilize sugar, proteins or fats to their fullest potential. Blood sugar levels may become dangerously low, resulting in hypoglycemia.

- Effects of Alcohol on the Heart

Alcohol is also a poison to muscle fibre, including heart muscle. Combined with vitamin deficiencies and other problems associated with alcohol use, the heart muscle can become weakened or destroyed. Anyone suffering from a heart condition will find that alcohol makes it worse and could precipitate a fatal heart attack.

Perhaps most significant is the effect of alcohol on blood pressure. Men and women who have a daily drinking routine, drinking more than three drinks a day, tend to have higher blood pressure than non-drinkers. Alcohol, therefore, has been included as a risk factor that can lead to hypertension. Doctors will often advise patients with high blood pressure to stop smoking and either stop or significantly decrease alcohol consumption.

- Effects of Alcohol on the Muscles

As described for the heart, alcohol weakens muscles. Muscle tremor, muscle incoordination and an increase in reaction time (i.e. the individual takes longer to react) occur. This is a very important factor to keep in mind when driving a car and operating machinery – *don't do it while under the influence of alcohol!*

- Effects of Alcohol on the Blood

Poor eating habits of the chronic alcohol user result in vitamin deficiencies. A drink often takes the place of a well-balanced meal. The resulting vitamin deficiencies have a profound effect on all parts and functions of the body. The list of medical blood problems resulting from alcohol abuse is long. A reduction in red blood cells (anemia), white blood cells and platelets have been reported, leading to an increased risk of infection and blood clotting problems.

- Effects of Alcohol on Hormone Levels

Alcohol produces a drop or fall in the male hormone, testosterone. Testosterone is the hormone responsible for the remarkable changes at puberty – transforming a boy into a man. Testosterone levels will usually return to normal fairly rapidly after the cessation of drinking; however, continued use produces consistently low levels of the hormone. In the male, this can produce female-like features such as breast growth, decreased body hair and reduced beard growth. In addition, there is decreased sexual drive and impotence. Prostate problems may also develop because the gland decreases in size and function is inhibited.

The effects to the female are equally serious but not as visibly evident. Alcohol does interfere with the menstrual cycle as a result of a change in ovarian function. The outcome might be sterility and an early onset of menopause.

- Effects of Alcohol on the Nervous System

Most people are aware of the effects on the nervous system when long-term use of alcohol is terminated. The symptoms of delirium tremens (DTs) are fairly well-known, as they have frequently been depicted by individuals in the movie industry. When drinking of alcohol stops, the substance that the body had grown accustomed to is no longer present. The reaction of the body is negative and initiates a host of unpleasant effects including trembling, excitement, anxiety, sweating, difficulty in sleeping, increased body temperature, increased heart rate and pain. These symptoms begin to occur two to four days after cessation of drinking or may result simply from a reduced blood alcohol level in the alcoholic who can't get his/her usual supply or is injured or catches an infection. The body is not able to handle the physical stress. A significant percentage of patients with DTs die.

Inflammation of nerves from continued alcohol consumption produces a burning and prickly sensation in the hands and feet. The actual cause is probably vitamin deficiency stemming from a poor diet. In fact, vitamin deficiencies are responsible for a number of the problems.

- Effects of Alcohol on the Brain

Serious brain damage by alcohol ingestion produces syndromes known as Wernicke syndrome and Korsakoff's psychosis, both of which are mental disorders. When one reaches the stage of Wernicke syndrome, drinking has been over an extended period of time (usually years). The Wernicke syndrome is characterized by confusion, difficulty in controlling eye and leg muscles and, if untreated, progresses to the more serious Korsakoff's psychosis which is characterized by memory loss. Psychosis means there is brain cell loss and damage to the brain structure. Korsakoff's psychosis is difficult to treat and might even be considered untreatable.

- Effects of Alcohol on the Mouth, Throat and Lungs

Continued use of alcohol increases the incidence of cancers of the mouth, throat and lungs. Cancers of these areas represent a significant proportion of all cancers detected in both white and black populations.

- Effects of Alcohol on Pregnancy

Alcohol, being a small molecule, readily crosses the placenta reaching the fetus and affecting development. Physical and mental deficiencies have been observed in newborns of mothers who continued to drink during pregnancy. These symptoms are collectively referred to as Fetal Alcohol Syndrome (FAS). Body size of the offspring is decreased compared to normal infants, the brain is smaller and there are varying degrees of mental retardation. Facial symptoms include abnormal growth of the jaw, an upturned nose, thin lips and abnormal facial skin folds. Heart defects (murmurs) have also been observed.

A woman who considers herself only a social or moderate drinker can still put the fetus at risk, but the symptoms are usually less severe than those seen with FAS. The fetus progresses through many developmental stages. Some of these stages are more sensitive to drugs, including alcohol, than other stages. The thalidomide tragedy is a good example of what a drug can do if taken at the wrong time during pregnancy. Many babies, born to mothers who took thalidomide during their pregnancy, had 'seal-like' appendages (flippers) rather than arms and hands. Many intricate processes occur during the development of the fetus. It is wise to avoid anything that might interfere with these

Alcohol and pregnancy – a dangerous combination.

stages. The best advice is to avoid drinking the 'simple drug' during pregnancy.

The use of alcohol has been linked to sexual behaviour and disinhibition. There certainly have been unwanted pregnancies resulting from sexual encounters while under the influence of alcohol. A study in Scotland showed that almost 50% of males and females had consumed alcohol before their first experience of sexual intercourse and those who had taken a drink were much less likely to have used condoms. Thus, alcohol could be considered a risk factor with respect to AIDS and other sexually transmitted diseases.

Tolerance and Dependence

As alcohol intake continues, the body adapts to and desires more alcohol in order to produce the effect felt with that first drink. This phenomenon is known as developing 'tolerance'. Individuals adapt to the continued depressant effects on the brain and gradually more alcohol is required before one appears drunk.

As with other drugs, both physical and psychological dependence to alcohol develops. Physical dependence is seen, in its worst scenario, as delirium tremens. As described in the case study at the beginning of this chapter on alcohol, Brad was physically dependent. When one feels that he/she must have the drug in order to survive or to be 'on top of things', psychological dependence has occurred.

Underage Drinking

An adult male takes between 7 to 15 years to become an alcoholic while an adult female takes between 5 and 12 years. Unfortunately, young people become alcoholics much quicker. The average time is between 2 to 5 years; however, some have become alcoholics in just a few months.

> *Alcoholism has been defined as 'a chronic disorder in which the individual is unable, for physical or psychological reasons, or both, to refrain from frequent consumption of alcohol in quantities sufficient to produce intoxication and ultimately, injury to health and functioning'.*

Treatment centres are now admitting significantly more teenage alcoholics. A young developing body simply has difficulty handling alcohol. As pointed out earlier, growing tissues and cells are more prone to the cellular poison (alcohol) than are mature adult tissues. Unfortunately, after people reach the so called 'magic age' when it is legal to drink, a significant number still cannot handle alcohol, but society is saying you now should be able to make your own wise decisions and society feels you are mature enough to make the right choice.

Young people have many reasons for drinking: curiosity, peer pressure, as a crutch during emotional upheavals and yes, because they want to behave like an adult.

What kind of message are adults giving young people? Is there any thought given to the consequences of their actions? How about graduation parties? Do the parties include alcohol, even though the students are underage? If so, why? Is it a fear of not being 'cool' or of being ridiculed? These parties create further peer pressure. Students are being pressured into attending a party which they normally might not attend simply because no alternatives are provided. The stage is set for a young person to drink. No one wants to be left out or feel like they don't belong!

If parents do not realize it is possible to celebrate without alcohol, the battle against alcohol abuse will never be won. There have been some landmark legal cases in which alcohol providers were found legally responsible for having served someone beyond the point of intoxication. The individual injured him or herself, or someone else, and sued for damages. The majority of these cases involved bars, restaurants or other licensed commercial establishments, but anyone who provides alcohol is potentially liable. In fact, a 1996 Alberta court decision indicates that a non-commercial host must take reasonable steps to prevent injury to third parties by inebriated guests, especially teenage guests. This is serious! Parents in North America who have taken the challenge and who have worked hard in creating drug-free parties for youth are to be commended.

Is alcohol a 'simple' drug? The evidence has been in for some time and the answer is **NO!**

LET'S SEE WHAT YOU'VE LEARNED ABOUT ALCOHOL

Is it okay to drink alcohol as a teenager?

Where in the body does alcohol go when it is absorbed from the stomach/small intestine?

How much alcohol does it take to affect judgement and self-control?

What are some of the effects of chronic use of alcohol?

MARIJUANA

WHAT'S THE 'DOPE'?

MARIJUANA

What's The 'Dope'?

The terminology 'gone to pot', although often used to describe the physical shape of our bodies, can quite appropriately be used to describe those who have begun using *marijuana*. There are over 200 slang terms for marijuana, including 'pot', 'herb', 'weed', 'boom', 'chronic', and 'gangster'. The use of marijuana has been extensively documented for years but only recently have the harmful effects on the body received attention. Serious physical, psychological or mind-altering effects are now being reported with regular and chronic use.

The following cases describe some of the serious effects of marijuana.

> *Tom, an attractive, well-mannered, intelligent grade 10 student, was liked by both his teachers and fellow students. His younger brother, Jim, fit a similar description except he was in grade 8. Both were very involved in school and community sports including hockey, soccer, baseball and football. To everyone's dismay, at Christmas time in grade 11, Tom was expelled from school for his involvement in a drug distribution ring that operated within his school. Tom's specific involvement was the distribution of marijuana and its products, namely hashish oil (the more concentrated form of the plant) and hashish cubes, as well as plant material itself, to his fellow classmates. The distribution system was so widespread that no other school in the city, including private schools, would accept Tom as a student, as they were all aware of his activities. Consequently, Tom never finished high school. Tom had come under suspicion when his grades began to drop with no identifiable cause. The friends with whom he associated*

also changed over the summer holidays, developing a lack of respect for school authority. His attentiveness subsequently declined and he would show up late for classes or not show at all. Involvement in sports activities also dropped markedly. On the other hand, Jim remained in the background when it came to Tom's drug involvement. He participated only as a user rather than a distributor. Tom and Jim are now adults. Tom is not married and is working in construction. Jim also had a construction job, but is divorced and has a young daughter. Jim met his wife among a drug-using crowd. She became pregnant when both of them were heavily involved in marijuana use. Their daughter, Susan, when born, appeared to be a normal, bright, healthy baby and her first few years of growth appeared uneventful. Susan is now in school and is having difficulty learning and socializing. According to her teachers she tends to be a loner. Even her grandparents noticed a significant change in her attitude toward them. Tom continues to use marijuana products on a fairly regular basis, always striving to find the best available products, products of high quality and potency. He is no longer able to carry on an intelligent conversation.

Paul, a 20-year-old, had just recently graduated from Business Administration 'cum laude'. He had been working in the family business and, before his experience with marijuana, was well adjusted both in his job and social life. Although Paul only smoked marijuana twice during his college days, he soon found his way into the 'in' crowd and began to smoke regularly. This habit immediately began to produce changes in his working pattern and a decline in ambition. The situation worsened to the point of apathy and distrust of friends and family. Six months after starting to regularly smoke marijuana, Paul developed delusions of omnipotence ('holier than thou') and grandeur ('there is no one as good as I'). He believed he was in charge of the mafia and he was a necessary supporter of the

The potency of today's marijuana.

Ku Klux Klan. He began to collect guns and knives, and trained his German shepherd dog to attack others. Finally, for fear of losing his mind, Paul sought psychiatric treatment. Upon discontinuing the use of the drug his fantasies disappeared. However, two years following treatment, Paul was still experiencing some difficulty in thinking clearly.

David, an outgoing 19-year-old teenager, had many friends and did well academically. Following only four months of marijuana use, he experienced a sharp decline in his interest for schoolwork. He became listless, apathetic and depressed. He shunned family and friends and gradually developed ideas of reverence. Believing he had superhuman powers, he felt able to communicate with and control the minds and actions of animals, especially dogs and cats. Although he admitted these were weird ideas, he considered them to be true and believed marijuana was his source of power. Fortunately, when psychiatric help was sought and marijuana smoking discontinued, David returned to a level of functioning similar to that before marijuana use.

Each year, thousands of adolescents and adults experiment with marijuana with the false impression that it will do no harm. There is the belief that use can be controlled. Contrary to this popular belief, marijuana is indeed a dangerous drug and continued use could have serious consequences on the normal functioning of the body.

What is Marijuana?

Marijuana, hash (also known as hashish), and hash oil are all obtained from the Cannabis plant. The North American variety, Cannabis sativa, is a fibre-like plant with a well-recognized star-shaped leaf.

Over 400 chemicals have been found in the plant. The heat produced on smoking a marijuana cigarette ('joint') results in chemical reactions, which in turn produce an estimated total of 2,000 compounds. Unfortunately, the effects of all 2,000 compounds, when inhaled, are not known. It is frightening to even try to guess what the inhalation of 2,000 foreign compounds could do to the body. Over 60 of the 400 plus compounds found in a joint are collectively known as cannabinoids, the major one being THC (tetrahydrocannabinol or delta 9-THC). THC is the cannabinoid responsible for the 'high'. Related compounds, CBN (cannabinol) and CBD (cannabidiol), also have biological activity but the mind-altering effects are not like those obtained from THC.

The potency of marijuana bought on the streets is determined by the THC content. During the late 1960s and early 1970s, THC content was low – approximately one-half percent. In the 1980s, it was not uncommon to find marijuana containing as much as 8% to 9% THC. Some recent studies, in 2000, have reported levels of THC as high as 29.6%! In other words, marijuana today is much more potent and, more seriously, is being used by a younger age group. Just stop to think about it for a moment – public school children are inhaling 2,000 chemicals from a more potent plant source. Why, then, are there so many so-called 'experts' who want to decriminalize the 'weed'?

The increased level, or concentration, of THC in the marijuana plant is partially due to cross-breeding (similar to the process which gives better wheat crops) and improved growing techniques, including hydroponics (growing plants in nutrient solutions, with or without soil). Unfortunately, it is now possible to grow the plant in your home, garage or in some secluded spot, although the excess electricity consumption needed for the growing lights might raise the suspicion of authorities.

Although the dangers of using marijuana are often attributed to the THC content, there are other constituents that are of equal concern. These include the tar and cancer-causing constituents found in the joint. Cannabis smoking produces 50% more tar than the same weight of a popular tobacco brand cigarette. How many filter tip joints have you seen? The tar contains more than 150 polynuclear aromatic hydrocarbons, including the same cancer-causing agents found in cigarettes. One of these hydrocarbons is known as benzo[a]pyrene. The concentration of this component in marijuana tar is reportedly 70% higher than in the same weight of tobacco tar.

Methods of Marijuana Use

Marijuana is most often smoked as a 'joint'. The joint contains ground up plant material, leaves and seeds. In recent years marijuana has appeared in 'blunts', which are cigars that have been emptied of their tobacco and refilled with marijuana, often in combination with another drug, such as crack. Occasionally, marijuana is consumed by mixing it with foods. Brownies have been known to contain hashish. A number of years ago a cookbook appeared on the streets, which contained recipes requiring the inclusion of marijuana constituents. Interestingly, the book ended with a page explaining what to do if too much was consumed, i.e. a remedy for an overdose!

Marijuana is also used in the more concentrated form, 'hash' or 'hashish'. This concentrate, usually sold as a 'cube', is dark brown to black in colour and because it is a concentrated form, contains much higher levels of THC. Hashish is actually a resinous material secreted onto the surface of the plant. In some parts of the world, women used to be in charge of collecting this resin. Wearing leather aprons, they would run up and down the fields so that the resin would stick to the aprons. The resin would then be scraped off with a knife. This is, of course, not a very sanitary process. Hash and hash oil have frequently been used to lace cigarettes or joints. Hash is also smoked using a pipe (which may or may not be a water pipe) or a bong (a large diameter tube device used to mix air with the smoke thereby cooling the smoke prior to inhalation). Because the smoke from hash is very irritating to the throat, water or air is used to cool the smoke and relieve some of this irritation.

The highest concentration of THC is found in hash oil. This oil is obtained by percolation (a process similar to that used for making coffee in a drip-percolator). Injection of hash oil is not a common practice because this method poses serious health problems: blood clots (from foreign particles in the injected material) and numerous diseases as a result of using dirty needles and syringes. Injecting hash oil is truly 'Russian Roulette'! Hash oil has also been added to cigarettes or joints.

Marijuana Distribution in the Body

THC and the other cannabinoids found in the marijuana plant are highly fat soluble; that is, they behave like an oil. The cannabinoids rapidly enter fat tissues of the body, but leave the fat tissues very slowly! The term 'fat heads', although not a term of endearment, is really quite descriptive. Brain tissue is composed of considerable fat and marijuana 'loves' to spend time in this part (as well as other areas) of our bodies. Chronic or regular users of marijuana have been shown to have 50% or less brain cell energy than seen in individuals who have not used the

Marijuana migration to the brain.

drug. Because cells are surrounded with lipid (fat soluble) material, THC eventually buries itself within every cell in the body. THC actually buries itself between the molecules that make up the membranes. As marijuana intake continues, the pores within these membranes become clogged. Clogged cells have difficulty functioning properly. THC stays in the fat tissues for days. In fact, scientists have been able to detect constituents of marijuana in the body at least one month after smoking one joint. Thus, the weekend user is actually accumulating marijuana constituents in the body. This means that what was inhaled last Saturday hasn't completely left the body by the following Saturday!

Marijuana Effects on the Cell Function

In 1998, scientists discovered that the membranes of certain cells contain protein receptors that bind THC. Once securely in place, THC kicks off a series of cellular reactions that ultimately lead to the 'high' that users experience when they smoke.

The human body is composed of millions of cells. Human growth and development is dependent upon continual cellular growth and regeneration. THC and other cannabinoids inhibit this cellular growth rate by 8% to 55%, depending on the concentration found in the plant material. It is a well-known fact that growing cells are more prone to the toxic effects of chemicals than are mature cells. This means young people are particularly vulnerable, and damage to nervous system cells could be irreversible, i.e. these cells do not regenerate. On the other hand, some of the damage may be subtle, resulting in only minor defects that are not fatal to the cell. However, there are times when the cell actually dies or turns into a potential cancer cell.

Marijuana Effects on the Brain

THC changes the way in which sensory information gets into and is processed by the hippocampus. The hippocampus is a component of the brain's limbic system that is crucial for learning, memory, and the integration of sensory experiences with emotions and motivations. Investigations have shown that THC suppresses neurons in the information-processing system of the hippocampus, as well as the activity of the nerve fibres in this region. In addition, researchers have discovered that learned behaviours, which depend on proper functioning of the hippocampus, also deteriorate via this mechanism. Brain processes are inhibited and, to put it bluntly, the user becomes dumber and dumber with continued use! Long-term use produces changes in the brain similar to those seen after long-term use of other major drugs of abuse.

High-powered microscopic examination of brain tissue, taken during an autopsy, has shown that marijuana constituents accumulate in communication junctions between nerve cells. This slows down the flow of information and increases the distance between the nerve cells. This effect may be permanent. Regardless of how little or how infrequently one uses marijuana, it all 'adds up'. If used long enough, one may experience what is know as an Organic Brain Syndrome. This syndrome has many characteristic symptoms – lack of motivation, apathy and impairment of short-term memory. As a result, some have difficulty getting their lives back together after long-term use. We have only one brain. A brain scan of a marijuana user might be most convincing. Paul (see beginning of this chapter) had fuzzy thinking for two years after using the drug. This 'fuzzy' thinking was due, at least partially, to the accumulation of marijuana in the brain.

Because the user's thought process is slowed after using marijuana, under no circumstance should he/she drive a motor vehicle. A number of motor vehicle accidents have undoubtedly been caused by marijuana. Forensic laboratories have frequently found marijuana in the bodies of motor vehicle fatality victims. The Federal Government of Canada supported the establishment of a 'Drugs and Driving Committee' to look into the involvement of drugs and their effects on the ability to drive. One issue of particular interest to this committee is the involvement of marijuana in drug fatalities and injuries.

Cannabis Syndrome and Psycho-Social Effects

The effects of marijuana on the brain result in serious problems for the user. Doctors have reported seeing patients with decreased motivation, shortened attention and concentration spans, lack of interest in the world around them, a limited range of thought and feeling, an inability to prepare realistically for the future, unrealistic thinking, impaired communication skills and, above all, a general apathy. These symptoms have been coined the 'Cannabis Syndrome'. It is sad to see young people behave in this manner. Tremendous potential lies ahead of them and they 'could care less'! Because of this, it is not uncommon for these individuals to lose friends, drop out of school, lose jobs and fight with family members. Marijuana users could, very quickly, become an expense to society, as they do not function normally. It is very difficult to go back to school and try to catch up with material that should have been learned years back. It could become a vicious circle! Lack of education – no job!

Marijuana Effects on the Immune System

Marijuana impairs the functioning of 'T-cells'. These cells are important for normal functioning of the immune system. The AIDS virus kills 'T-cells' thereby leaving the individual susceptible to serious life-threatening complications. Marijuana not only affects the 'T-cells' but also 'B-cells' (cells which produce antibodies). With these two cell types impaired, the defence system of the body is severely hampered and the user has difficulty fighting infections.

Our bodies have a certain number of precancerous cells. Fortunately, our immune system recognizes these cells and destroys them. An impaired immune system obviously reduces the efficiency with which these precancerous cells are destroyed and thus increases the risk of developing cancer.

Marijuana Effects on the Reproductive System

Tissue surrounding the testes in the male is very high in fat content. Accumulation of marijuana constituents in this part of the body decreases the production of testosterone. It has been reported that levels of testosterone are decreased by as much as 35% within hours after smoking only one joint. Following the cessation of smoking, the testosterone levels will begin to return to normal unless the user is a chronic (continuous) smoker. The male who has not reached puberty will find the decrease in testosterone results in a delay in the development of secondary sex characteristics, such as the deepening of the voice, growth of body hair on the face, groin and armpit areas. Low testosterone levels may also result in enlargement of the breasts. This would likely prove embarrassing to most male egos.

Sperm production also decreases in those using marijuana. The decreased sperm count and motility of the sperm partially explain decreased fertility of the male marijuana user. Couples who want to have children may not be able to, but even more frightening is the possibility of transmitting defective genetic material from the male to the offspring.

Birth defects are a possibility. Remember, the father contributes one-half of the genes to the fetus!

The female is also affected by marijuana use. Ovaries have fat content much like that of the testes. The female hormones (estrogen and progesterone) levels are altered by marijuana. Hormone disruption may mean testosterone levels in the female may become disproportionally high, resulting in excess hair growth on her body and a deepening of her voice. The female menstrual cycle is often disrupted and anovulatory cycles (a time when an egg is not released by the ovaries) may result in temporary infertility.

The female begins life with one set of eggs that begin to mature at puberty. These eggs are very sensitive to chemical toxins and since the eggs are immature, they are more prone to toxic effects of chemicals. If damage occurs, it is permanent and may have an effect on any newborn the woman may have in later life. THC will cross the placenta and accumulate in the brain of the developing fetus. Is there anything more that has to be said?

Marijuana Effects on the Heart

Marijuana causes an increase in heart rate. For the healthy individual this is probably not serious. Those with heart problems will find marijuana makes matters worse. Blood pressure changes have also been reported; however, the long-term effects of marijuana on blood pressure are not known.

Marijuana Effects on the Pulmonary System

Because marijuana is most often smoked and inhaled there has been considerable investigation into its effect on the lungs. Marijuana smoke is usually deeply inhaled to allow for maximum absorption and effect. The lung damage caused by just 4 joints per week is reportedly equivalent to smoking 16 tobacco cigarettes per day!

Lung damage may first appear as a sore throat, sometimes referred to as 'hash throat'. Irritation of the bronchial lining, or mucosa, can lead to inflammation of the lungs (bronchitis). If bronchitis is not treated, this, along with excess mucus production, will lead to airway obstruction, emphysema (a disease that causes distension of the lung and frequently impairment of heart action) and permanent lung disease.

Marijuana & Driving

Scientific studies conducted by forensic laboratories reveal marijuana detection in the body fluids of drivers involved in fatal motor vehicle accidents and in those involved in impaired driving cases. What effect does marijuana use have on driving capabilities?

One study revealed a significant deterioration in reaction time in each of the marijuana user groups.

A study on "Marijuana and Driving in Real-Life Situations" concluded: it is evident that marijuana does have a detrimental effect on driving skills and performance in a restricted driving area and this effect is even greater under normal conditions of driving on city streets. Obviously the conditions of this study were controlled. The reactions and decisions at high speed are unknown (one could assume if these reactions were evident under controlled situations, they would be worse at high speeds). The individuals participating in this study missed traffic lights or stop signs, engaged in passing maneuvers without sufficient caution and had poor anticipation or handling of the vehicle with respect to traffic flow. It should be pointed out that this study was done using marijuana containing THC content of 0.7% (low dose) to 1.2% (high dose). The marijuana available today could easily be 10 times plus more potent with respect to the THC content.

A further review indicates that there is subjective impairment in marijuana users driving vehicles on city streets - particularly in the areas of judgement, care and concentration. Some of these effects began immediately after initiation of smoking and lasted for up to four hours. In another study, pilots were tested on a simulator and impairment was still noted 24 hours after exposure even though the subjects were unaware of any residual effects. As the dose of marijuana increases there is a dose-dependent decrease in mental and physical performance. This could be even more pronounced in regular marijuana users since THC is stored in fat tissues and thus accumulates in the body.

A study of 58 subjects who smoked marijuana joints until they felt "high" were tested periodically by highway patrol officers on roadside sobriety tests. It should not be any surprise that 94% of them failed to pass the sobriety test 90 minutes after smoking and 60% failed after 150 minutes even though the plasma concentrations were rather low. In fact, plasma THC levels may not reflect ability since THC is fat soluble and rapidly leaves the blood to enter tissues.

In most individuals the social use of marijuana produces a sense of well-being (euphoria), a pleasant state of relaxation, altered perception, particularly of distance and time, impaired short-term memory and impaired physical coordination. The state of intoxication is usually mild and short-lived (2-3 hours after one joint). A 'high' may have serious consequences if the user attempts to drive, fly, or operate heavy machinery during the state of intoxication. It is now well recognized that even low doses of marijuana adversely affect driving performance due to a complex interaction of changes in reaction time, in judgement and in perception of sensory stimuli and time.

In humans, depending on the make-up of the individual, cannabis may produce panic or anxiety reactions. These could obviously affect driving ability! The anxiety reactions do not outlast the length of the cannabis intoxication (2-4 hours).

In summary, it is known that individuals, after smoking marijuana, are pre-occupied with their inner thoughts (as one paper points out - marijuana increases the consciousness of one's inner thoughts and mental processes and thus decreases one's consciousness of external stimuli) and thus are not in full control of the task they are undertaking. This appears true in the case of driving. For this reason there would probably be some risk-taking, although it may not be intentional. Driving has been shown to be impaired in a number of studies and the impairment has been detected for hours after one joint.

Marijuana can hardly be considered a drug that is safe to use. The 'dope' on this drug shows that use may lead to permanent damage not only to the user, but possibly to their offspring. The drug has been inappropriately referred to as a 'soft' drug. The health effects on the human body are not soft! **Don't let yourself 'go to pot'** as the consequences of this **'dope'** could be serious!

LET'S SEE WHAT YOU'VE LEARNED ABOUT MARIJUANA

What are the various types of marijuana products that are abused?

How many chemicals are found in the marijuana plant?

Has the potency of marijuana changed since the 1960s?

Where is marijuana stored in the body?

What are some possible serious health effects associated with marijuana use?

COCAINE

ALL IS NOT GOLD

COCAINE
All Is Not Gold

If a single drug was regarded as the 'drug of the 1980s', it would have to be cocaine. Unfortunately, its use did not stop in the 1980s. Cocaine initially was the drug of the elite – it was considered a sign of wealth. This is not the case anymore. Many segments of society, including the poor, have succumbed to cocaine. Unfortunately, the dangers of cocaine use have not been adequately portrayed. The movie industry has glamorized the drug and should be held accountable for falsifying the real effects. The drug does kill. Death can occur suddenly and without warning. Unlike gold, life does not have any glitter if hooked on cocaine.

The following cases depict the dangers associated with cocaine use.

> *Ron, a 25-year-old male, experienced convulsions after intravenous cocaine use. He had been abusing the drug an average of three times a day for about eight months. Although the majority of his cocaine abuse involved snorting the drug, he was able to develop an intravenous form of administration, which he used during the last month. At about six o'clock in the morning he was admitted to hospital; he had injected two 'dimes' (about 140 mg) of the drug. He instantly felt dizzy and fell to the floor. His mother arrived shortly and noticed Ron was convulsing. Ron appeared confused but alert when seen later at the hospital.*

> *Lisa, a 21-year-old female, went with a group of friends to a party. After drinking several cocktails she snorted a white powder believed to be cocaine. She soon experienced convulsions and was quickly taken to the hospital. Unfortunately, Lisa failed to respond to treatment and died forty minutes after admission. Several other people at the party admitted using the same substance but denied having any bad experiences.*

> *Jeff, a 28-year-old male, was seen using drugs on the day of his death. He had been drinking early in the evening and smoked two pipes of hashish. Shortly after midnight, Jeff began to snort cocaine and continued to do so periodically for 2 hours before he collapsed. A friend called the fire department and Jeff was rushed to the nearest hospital but was pronounced dead on arrival. A small vial found near his body contained a white powder – cocaine.*

> *Susan, a 19-year-old female, came to the hospital complaining of chest pain. She told the doctor the pain appeared suddenly and that she had no idea what the cause could be. Upon further questioning she admitted to snorting cocaine just prior to getting the chest pain. Fortunately, very little damage was done to the lungs and she did not require hospitalization.*

The dangerous effects resulting from cocaine use came to the forefront with the death of the basketball star, Len Bias, in June 1986. The first draft pick of the Boston Celtics was dead! His death occurred just twelve hours after signing a ten-year multimillion dollar contract. Traces of cocaine were found in Bias' urine. Other athletes have also been affected and more are now coming forward to tell of their experiences with the drug.

Cocaine is the most addicting drug available today. Once use is started it is hard to 'kick the habit'. The drug literally takes over your life! Darryl Strawberry, the New York Yankees designated hitter, was suspended for a year in early 2000. He was suspended twice previously for cocaine use, and tested positive again. The drug literally takes over your life! Nothing else matters! Some former users have described it as the 'King and Queen' of all drugs.

How Cocaine is Used

Cocaine is used in a number of ways. The drug is often **sniffed or inhaled ('snorted')** through the mucous membranes of the nose. A 'high' occurs in less than a minute. If continued, nasal problems develop since cocaine is a vasoconstrictor. This means it constricts the blood vessels in the nose. Constriction decreases blood flow resulting in inadequate nourishment. With continued use, inadequate nourishment results in ulcer formation in the nasal septum (that portion of the nose which separates the two nostrils) and, if not treated soon enough, could eventually lead to a hole developing in the septum. Some addicts think it is 'cool' to put a handkerchief in one nostril and pull it out the other – real magic. Metal plates for replacement of the septum are available for purchase – an indication of the prevalence of this effect.

Cocaine may also be **injected.** The drug, upon entering the vein, will travel to the heart increasing the heartbeat, causing chest pain and heart attacks in some individuals. Disposable syringes are used for injection of the drug, sometimes along with toilet bowl water. Toilet bowl water is often used for dissolving drugs as abusers have to 'do drugs' privately to avoid being caught.

'Freebasing' cocaine involves the inhalation of cocaine vapours. Commercially, cocaine is available as a salt. The salt portion of the drug is removed by a simple chemical reaction. The 'free base' (that is, cocaine minus the salt) is extracted with an organic solvent, such as ether, and then heated to vaporize the drug. Inhalation of the drug in this manner is like injecting the drug without a needle.

The History of Cocaine

Cocaine is an alkaloid (a common chemical class of basic compounds) obtained from the leaves of the plant *Erythroxylum coca*. The leaves contain varying concentrations of cocaine in addition to 18 other substances. For many years, the local inhabitants of countries such as Peru were known to chew the leaves of this plant, supposedly to obtain strength and vigour. Although coca leaves were introduced to Europe by explorers, coca chewing was regarded as a barbaric Indian practice by Europeans. It wasn't until cocaine was isolated from the leaves that interest in the drug became more widespread.

The use of cocaine, for purposes other than medical, began in Europe with the production of a French wine known as *Vin Mariani,* which contained cocaine. The wine was considered to be a sign of social prestige because it was used by members of the upper class. In 1886, a second beverage containing cocaine was manufactured. This new mixture, named Coca-Cola®, became very popular in North America. In 1906, the Coca-Cola Company agreed to stop using cocaine in the drink. Cocaine is now extracted from the leaves, turned over to the government laboratories for medical purposes and the de-cocainized leaves (without cocaine) are used as a flavouring agent.

Recreational Use of Cocaine

Cocaine, as a street drug, is referred to as 'coke', 'snow', 'C', 'lady', 'she', 'girl', 'toot', 'nose candy', 'white girl' and 'white lady'. Cocaine users traditionally were affluent people with large amounts of money. To prove their wealth they would often snort the drug (inhale through the nostrils), using a gold-plated straw or a rolled-up $100 bill. Today cocaine users are not only your stereotype movie stars but also blue collar workers, paper boys, students and, in fact, people from just about every walk of life. Affluence is no longer a criteria.

Street cocaine comes in one of the following forms: coca leaf, coca paste, cocaine hydrochloride powder, freebase cocaine, or crack. Coca leaf is considered the milder product because the cocaine content is low and it is chewed. This form of cocaine use is not popular in North America because coca plants do not grow in North American climates and the leaves are hard to smuggle through customs.

Coca paste is one of the first products obtained on extraction of the coca leaves. A 'high' is quickly obtained if the substance is smoked by adding it to a tobacco cigarette or marijuana joint. The substance is very addicting and has created nightmares for drug treatment workers. In Third World countries, children have become addicted to the paste in a matter of days. Attempts at treatment have not been successful. After release from the treatment facility, the person just has to get a whiff of burning coca paste and they're off on their abuse pattern again. Because the paste is impure, the cost of the substance is low when compared to the cocaine hydrochloride powder.

The hydrochloride salt is the most common form of cocaine sold on the street. This form is also used medicinally for certain types of surgery (eye, nose), as it is an effective local anesthetic, causing a numbness of the affected area. With illegal use of cocaine, the powder is most often taken by snorting fine lines of the drug through the nasal passages or by injecting a solution of the salt into a vein. A variety of strengths of the salt are available. These strength differences are a result of 'cutting' the salt with agents such as glucose, mannitol or lactose. Sometimes the cutting agents also have an effect on the body. Typical cutting agents include caffeine, lidocaine (see story of Lisa at the beginning of this chapter) and procaine (another local anesthetic). Street samples analyzed by laboratories have been found to contain anywhere from 0% to 90% cocaine. A lot of street purchasers get 'ripped off', paying dearly for something they did not get.

Attempts to remove the cutting agents in order to enhance the effects of the cocaine are accomplished by chemical manipulation and freebasing. Highly flammable solvents, which have a nasty tendency to explode and burst into flames, are used to extract the free base, yielding pure cocaine. Freebasing is a dangerous practice. The famous comedian Richard Pryor severely burned himself while freebasing. The line sometimes heard, 'it's okay to freebase if you don't get burned', is simply not true.

Crack

A recent method of freebasing is the instant 'ready-to-use' form of cocaine known as 'crack' (not to be confused with 'crank', an amphetamine derivative). Crack is obtained by a simple chemical reaction on the salt, cocaine hydrochloride. The resulting product is in the form of 'rocks', which are often distributed in small plastic vials. The vials are priced between $10 and $20, a factor that has made them extremely popular. The rocks are put into a pipe, lit and the resulting smoke is inhaled. The cracking noise produced on heating these rocks is the reason the product has been given the name 'crack'. Crack houses have appeared in many of the major cities of the United States. In Canada, crack has not gained the same popularity, possibly due to the advanced warning from the United States and the tremendous education provided both in classrooms and by the media. Smoking crack produces an instant exhilarating feeling. The higher the euphoria, the deeper the depression when the effects of the drug wear off. The user

Crack has its hazards.

knows how to obtain that 'good' feeling again – by using more crack – thus, addiction is rapid!

Cocaine Effects on the Body

When cocaine is snorted, it is absorbed through the mucous membranes lining the inside of the nose. Once absorbed through the membranes, cocaine goes to the heart, increasing heartbeat, causing chest pain and heart attacks in some instances (see stories at the beginning of the chapter). In fact, the cardiac arrhythmias (variations from normal rhythm of the heartbeat) produced by the drug are responsible for most of the deaths – too much stimulation! From the heart, the drug goes to the lungs, effectively decreasing exercise tolerance; that is, the user is unable to tolerate as much exercise as they once could. Cocaine then goes back to the heart and ultimately to the brain. The effects on the brain are on par with human survival factors, namely, food, water and sex. The drug takes the place of these necessary components in the users' lives. Cocaine effects are the most reinforcing of any drug known to man.

Cocaine interrupts and interferes with the normal functioning of chemicals naturally present in the brain. Normally, these chemicals are kept in balance and are required for specific functions. When needed by the body, they are released from storage sites, attach to receptors and initiate the chemical reactions the brain intended to perform. The process is much like plugging an electrical appliance into a power outlet. The appliance will not function until the plug has been attached to the electrical outlet (receptor). Once the need for the appliance is finished, it is simply unplugged or the power is turned off. Similarly, in the brain, once the need for the chemical has been satisfied, the power, so to speak, is turned off and the excess chemical is taken back to the storage site by a 'reuptake' pump process. Unfortunately, cocaine interferes with the functioning of this 'reuptake' process. It fills the cavities in this pump so that the excess brain chemical cannot be returned to the original storage site. Since the pump is full, it cannot retrieve the brain chemical. Dopamine is one of the chemicals produced by the brain and is seriously affected by cocaine use. Cocaine use results in the release of dopamine from its storage sites. As cocaine use is continued, dopamine is continually released until the storage sites are empty. It's like squeezing a lemon – eventually it becomes dry. Too little dopamine produces Parkinson-like effects. The user begins to shake – it's no wonder ballplayers can't hit a ball and their batting averages bottom-out after using this drug. The brain craves dopamine. Cocaine users take more of the drug in an attempt to squeeze more dopamine out of the storage sites. Eventually there is no more to squeeze. The effects are obviously devastating.

On initial use, cocaine acts quickly producing a short euphoric state (feels like you are floating on 'cloud nine') during which the user may experience feelings of great power and over-alertness. The individual does not feel tired; in fact, he/she feels like they could 'go' for days. Sometimes the user will turn to other drugs to counteract these symptoms. For example, sedatives (sleeping pills, alcohol, barbiturates etc.) are used to get some sleep. As the effects of cocaine begin to wear off, depression sets in. The addict may sleep for days, may become anxious and even suicidal if more cocaine cannot be obtained. With frequent use of the drug, the addict can become paranoid, over-suspicious and even experience hallucinations. Unpleasant hallucinations include the sensation of bugs crawling under the skin. Some physicians describe these effects as follows:

> *"The characteristic of their hallucinations is an arousal of a sensation of foreign bodies under the skin. The first patient scrapes his tongue and imagines seeing small black worms coming out of it. He also looks into the cavities to pull out the cholera microbes. The second patient tears off his skin again, looking in the bottom of the wound to pull out the microbes with his fingernails or with the point of a pin. The third....occupies himself looking for crystals of cocaine under his skin."*

Although hallucinations usually develop after months or years of cocaine use, the paranoia and hallucinations can last for days.

Injection or freebasing cocaine produces the same type of effects on the body as described above with snorting. Injecting implies the use of disposable syringes (often shared and are a major contributing cause of illnesses, including AIDS) and sometimes toilet bowl water to dissolve the drug. A 'high' is obtained within 14 seconds. Intravenous cocaine use may also cause extensive skin damage.

Four days after injection of one-half gram of cocaine into the left arm vein, a 35-year-old man appeared at a physician's office with an infected site on his thighs, an infection that had actually caused cell death. The man had reported that within four minutes after injection of the cocaine he had intense thigh pain and discolouration, followed by bruising and blistering of the area several hours later. He also had a fever and inflammation of the kidney and liver (hepatitis). Investigation showed that the intravenous cocaine had produced clots in the vessels of the skin, which restricted blood flow to that area. This effect was due to the cocaine itself and not any of the cutting agents. The severe pain following injection could be attributed to the intense vasoconstrictive properties (causing constriction of blood vessels) of cocaine, while the skin damage could be due either to prolonged constriction or the direct toxic effects of what was an overdose of cocaine.

Inhaling the vapours during freebasing or smoking crack gives instant euphoria. Incidentally, there are 'five star freebase chefs' for hire! They reportedly prevent one from getting burned!

Tolerance and Dependence

It is now known that cocaine use does produce tolerance (more drug is required in order to get the original effect) and dependence. In animal experiments, cocaine was administered by having the animal press a lever. In some cases, these animals would self-administer more than 4000 injections of cocaine to a point of severe toxicity and self-mutilation. Monkeys have continued administration until they went into convulsions and died. A similar psychological dependence develops in humans after continued use. Will-power and psychological maturity will not protect an individual from addiction. Soon the large quantities and high costs of the drug result in financial ruin and possibly lead to crime in order to support the habit.

Reverse tolerance is also thought to occur in humans. The process involves a sensitization of the individual to cocaine. This means the body requires smaller amounts of drug instead of more to produce the same degree of euphoria. The great danger in reverse tolerance is that the addict has already built up a high degree of dependence to cocaine and is using high doses of the drug. All of a sudden, the body recognizes this high dose as too much and the user goes into seizures and may die.

Cocaine and Driving

Cocaine users, after an extended period of use, often become paranoid. In fact, suspicion, distrust and paranoia are symptoms reported by cocaine smokers and snorters. This paranoia obviously can have a profound effect on driving ability. The following illustrates how paranoia affects driving.

> *Paranoid to begin with, and constantly suspicious, dealers get erratic if they feel they're being watched. Some will drive ten miles an hour in a fifty-mile zone, then do eighty miles an hour in a ten-mile zone. If this doesn't reveal unwelcome company, the cocaine dealer still will not relax. Far from it! He might run three or four red lights, hoping this will lure surveillance out of hiding. Some dealers will speed around the block three times, stop the car, get out and wave their arms in the air for what seems to be no particular reason at all, except that they are paranoid!*

The following illustrates the effects of cocaine on driving. It's frightening to think there are people, high on cocaine, behind the wheel of a vehicle.

> *A 30-year-old male, with a two-year history of social cocaine use, had been in a treatment program where he abstained from the drug for 90 days. He reported receiving a gift of one gram of cocaine, which he snorted over the weekend. The following day, a craving for more cocaine overwhelmed him. This was accompanied by depression and suicidal thoughts. Desperate for help, he drove at a high speed to a local treatment centre. During the drive he collided head-on with another vehicle, drove from the scene while being pursued, hit a second car that was parked, then exited his own car and ran away.*

In North America, it is not uncommon to find cocaine in the blood of drivers involved in fatal motor vehicle accidents. Unfortunately, these individuals are not always just on cocaine. Many had been drinking and since cocaine is a stimulant, they did not feel the depressant effects of alcohol and, therefore, drank to excess.

Cocaine and Pregnancy

Cocaine abuse by pregnant women significantly reduces birth weight, increases the stillbirth rate and increases the risk of congenital malformations. The infants also experience considerable stress at birth due to withdrawal from cocaine. The fetus had been participating in the drug habit of their mother since cocaine passes the placental barrier. At birth, the infant is no longer receiving 'their drug' and they experience withdrawal symptoms. If the physician or nursing staff is not aware of the drug-taking habits of the mother, it may be some time before appropriate measures can be taken to relieve the infant from his/her distress.

As recently as 1980, cocaine was said to be relatively safe, non-addicting and would only cause minor psychological problems. Nothing could be further from the truth! Although the movie industry has glamorized cocaine use, we now know there is nothing glamorous about the drug. The happy times depicted are short-lived. This is hard for our youth to rationalize abstinence when they see or hear about their so-called idols using the drug. Cocaine ruins lives, careers, family units and the purpose for living. Death is a possibility either from an overdose (sometimes due to reverse tolerance), a paranoia that leads to suicide, or from a traffic fatality. Cocaine is very addicting. **ALL THAT GLITTERS IS NOT GOLD!** The choice is obviously up to the individual. If alive, Len Bias would tell us to not experiment with cocaine or any of its products.

LET'S SEE WHAT YOU'VE LEARNED ABOUT COCAINE

Why do ulcers form in the nose when cocaine is snorted?

Why is crack so addicting?

What do you understand by the term 'reverse tolerance'?

Why do some cocaine users develop Parkinson-like effects?

What are some of the other health effects of cocaine use?

INHALATION ABUSE

IT'S BETTER TO 'STOP AND SMELL THE ROSES'

INHALATION ABUSE
It's Better To 'Stop And Smell The Roses'

The concept of the old popular song 'Stop and Smell the Roses' was good advice. Unfortunately, some started smelling or inhaling other things that have led to serious and life-threatening problems. Consider the following:

> *The body of an 8-year-old boy, Craig, was found frozen and tangled in a barbed wire fence. The only clue as to the cause of death was traces of a white substance in his nostrils. He had been sniffing typewriter correction fluid.*

> *Ted, a 16-year-old boy, sat in a field with three other boys sniffing a cleaning fluid from a plastic bag. After 45 minutes of intermittent sniffing he jumped up, took off at a fast run for about 150 feet and then collapsed. He was pronounced dead on arrival at the hospital.*

> *Mark, a 16-year-old male, sprayed a deodorant into a plastic bag and took several deep breaths from the bag. He removed the bag from his face, grabbed one of his companions and said, "Help me! Help me!" then collapsed. He was rushed to a local hospital where attempts at resuscitation were unsuccessful.*

Sudden deaths associated with 'sniffing' emphasize the seriousness of this type of abuse. There is such a fine line between inhaling enough solvent to obtain a 'high' and inhaling too much and passing into unconsciousness. Common household products containing volatile solvents such as lacquer thinners, glues, nail polish remover, plastic cement and cooking sprays are capable of sensitizing the heart to a normal body chemical, epinephrine. Emotional and/or physical stress can cause the body to release extra amounts of epinephrine. This extra epinephrine makes the heart beat faster to the point where it cannot cope. Without medical treatment, the end result could be death due to fibrillation (rapid, randomized contractions of the heart). The heart does not have enough time to properly fill with blood and thus, delivery of blood to the other parts of the body is critically hampered.

The Problem in Perspective

Although sniffing or inhaling solvents is not new, the problem has spread since the first reports in the late 1950s. Serious physical and social problems can and do occur. For example, model cement inhalation can cause minor eye, nose and throat irritations, but more seriously, muscle weakness that could lead to tremors, nervous system breakdown, liver, kidney and brain damage, and heart abnormalities. In short, the most important organs of our body are seriously affected. Gasoline sniffing may result in hallucinations, anemias (where the blood forming functions of the body are seriously damaged) and even psychosis (where an individual thinks people are 'out to get him/her'). The problems that occur are all serious but depend to some extent on the product being inhaled. Each of the products used by inhalers contains different solvents or mixtures of solvents. From time to time, manufacturers change the formula used for manufacturing their products. Sniffers are obviously not made aware of the changes and have suddenly become ill and had to be hospitalized after sniffing the changed formulation.

Solvent abusers become lazy, apathetic and preoccupied with obtaining a 'high'. Nothing else matters! Poor academic performance becomes evident. Their group of friends will probably change, if they have any at all. The person becomes totally frustrated! Unfortunately, abusers do not always understand why things are going so poorly. They not only perform poorly in school but they get into trouble with the law and have trouble coping with personal problems. Despite the serious physical and social problems, governments have not developed a universal method for the control of the inhalation practice. Some merchants are forbidden to sell volatile products to minors yet in other parts of North America, such action is not enforced. Consequently, we

Is this the end?

find solvent abusers continually being referred for treatment and rehabilitation. Some of the young people being treated have also indicated a lot of 'sniffing' among their peers. There are parents who encourage and instruct their children to purchase or steal solvents for the family. Innocent victims are also being affected. Take, for example, a report of an infant being sedated with a solvent-dipped cloth, placed over the face, so the parents could sniff and drink in peace.

Solvent abuse has no respect for age, occupation or status. In some areas, it has been estimated the prevalence of solvent use varies between 3.8% and 16.6% of the population. The lower the age and the grade, the greater the number of users! For instance, one study found 12.1% of seventh graders used solvents while only 1.4% of thirteenth graders reported use.

Effects of Sniffing

Sniffing or inhaling solvents is hazardous. Sniffers desire a state of euphoria, or simply a 'high', but could rapidly lose consciousness and develop serious breathing problems with resulting damage to the brain and other body tissues. All of these factors may lead to death. The inhalation response develops progressively in four stages:

Stage 1: this excitatory stage gives one the feeling of 'floating on cloud nine'. However, some experience dizziness, visual and auditory hallucinations, drooling, nausea, vomiting, flushed skin, intolerance to light and bizarre behaviour.

Stage 2: symptoms include confusion, disorientation, dullness, loss of self-control, ringing in the ears, blurred vision, double vision, cramps, headache and loss of pain sensation.

Stage 3: there is further reduction in arousal and coordination. The abuser will appear dazed, dopey and drowsy. There is muscular incoordination, slurred speech and depressed reflexes.

Stage 4: the sniffer may be in a state of stupor, delirium, or unconsciousness, and may have bizarre dreams and epileptic-like seizures.

Obviously Stage 1 is as far as sniffers would like to go – at least for the excitatory part of this stage. Unfortunately, some do not stop here.

Long-Term Effects

The harmful effects of long-term solvent abuse have not been clearly defined. However, a number of complications have been seen. These include brain, kidney and liver damage, blood changes, and nervous system damage. Some abusers have had such serious nervous system effects that they became quadriplegic and will spend the rest of their lives in wheelchairs. Brain damage has been seen in both adults and children. An example of brain damage was seen in a 41-year-old woman who was admitted to hospital because she was 'losing her mind'.

For eight months, prior to admission, she had sniffed leaded gasoline three or four times a day. She would place her nose into the opening of a can containing the gasoline and inhale in an intermittent manner so that unconsciousness was avoided. She experienced a number of pleasant, as well as terrifying events. She began to hallucinate and thought she was being used for brain experiments. She was convinced men had placed radar in her home to spy on her thoughts. She frequently had terrifying dreams and would awaken screaming that blood was oozing from her scalp.

You Can Get Burned!

Along with the serious problems to the body resulting from inhalation, a number of sniffers have suffered burn injuries from gasoline and smoking. Consider the following two cases.

> *A 14-year-old girl was sniffing gasoline with friends in a car parked in front of her home. While she was holding the gasoline container between her legs one friend lit a cigarette. This caused an explosion, which resulted in serious burns to all of the occupants of the car.*

> *A 14-year-old boy skipped school and went with a friend to a wooded area to sniff gasoline. His friend bumped into him, causing some gasoline to spill on his clothing. Upon lighting a cigarette his body became a human torch!*

TOLERANCE: One tube isn't enough.

Fads of the 1990s

In the 1990s we saw an increase in butane and propane use. These substances can freeze the back of throat, cause edema (collection of fluid) and cut off the airway, i.e. they choke to death or suffocate. Literature reports reveal serious problems with cigarette lighter fluid abuse and abuse of the propane used in barbeques. One unlucky fellow was sniffing propane in his living room. He lit a cigarette, causing an explosion that literally lifted the roof of the house. As police tried to pull him from his home he was so badly burned that skin was pulled out before the individual. Fortunately, he survived but the result was a badly scarred body. In some parts of the Northern Canada, you can be fined if your barbeque propane gas tank is not secured with a chain and a lock (the fine could be as high as $10,000).

Tolerance to Solvents

Many children have reported the development of tolerance to solvent fumes. This means more of the product is needed to achieve the effect felt on the first experience. For instance, one boy needed to inhale the vapours from 25 tubes of glue in order to achieve the effect he originally got from one tube. Another abuser was rescued after using 56 tubes of glue. This tolerance phenomenon is costly, from a financial perspective, and could lead to crime or prostitution in order to support the habit. If a tube of model cement costs $1.95, the boys using 25 and 56 tubes of glue would need between $48 and $109 for each sniffing session. This amount of money is considerably more than an average child's allowance! More importantly, why settle for glue when you can purchase crack cocaine for much less? Glue sniffers have been known to progress to other drugs of abuse.

Products Used

Besides gasoline, retailers indicate the products most often abused include model airplane glue, contact cements and adhesives, nail polish remover, aerosols, Lysol® spray and hair sprays. Retail outlets report these products are difficult to keep in stock and the reason for their depletion is believed to be abuse. Other products such as deodorants, lighter fluid, spot removers, paint thinners, correction fluid and Rush (a volatile nitrite) are believed to be less commonly abused, but virtually any product which contains a volatile solvent has been or will be abused.

It is encouraging to note that 66% of retailers surveyed in a recent study thought they had an obligation to inform the public of the dangers of solvent-containing products. Unfortunately, a minority was found to be 'cashing-in' on the problem. In one community, one business was taking advantage of the solvent abuse situation by giving customers an extra can of Lysol® spray as an incentive to shop at their store.

Volatile Nitrites

Popping volatile nitrites by breaking their containers and sniffing them is also a popular fad. In the late 1960s, sales of amyl nitrite (a blood vessel dilator) rose sharply due to its nonmedicinal use as an agent for getting 'high' and as a substance for increasing sexual desire. The crushable amyl nitrite glass containers became known as 'poppers' to the drug culture and in the late 1970s, other nitrites (e.g. butyl nitrites) became so popular that they accounted for sales of $50 million per year. These nitrites, sold as over-the-counter room deodorizers, are commonly known by names like 'Rush', 'Macho', 'Aroma of Men', 'Locker Room', 'Bullet', 'Double Blast' and 'Thrust'. They are inhaled directly from the bottle or by means of a single or double nasal inhaler. Some discotheques used to use special lighting effects to indicate they were about to spray nitrite fumes over the dance floor. This practice supposedly promoted a sense of abandon in dancing and stimulated music appreciation. Ecstasy use at raves has now taken over for this practice.

Chemically, nitrites are very unstable. Decomposition occurs at room temperature or if exposed to daylight. The nitrites, when inhaled or ingested, can readily induce changes in the ability of blood to carry oxygen, due to an alteration in hemoglobin, resulting in the formation of methemoglobin. Users may become cyanotic and their skin may take on a bluish colour. Nitrites also cross the placental barrier in pregnant women and can produce blood changes in the fetus. Other toxic effects include: 'nitrite headaches', light-headedness, fainting, tolerance, lack of muscle control, delirium, a profound drop in blood pressure, skin flushing and transient heart changes. More seriously, inhaled nitrites are broken down in the body to a nitrite ion. This ion is a potential cancer-causing substance. Nitrites are also known to be immunosuppressant agents and can render the body more susceptible to infection.

Nitrous Oxide

Inhalation of nitrous oxide for a pleasurable experience is not uncommon. The oxide has been referred to as a 'bag full of laughs', the 'grocery-store high' and the 'lunch-hour drug'. When 'head shops' were legal, a proprietor of a shop in Toronto viewed nitrous oxide as the ideal mind-altering substance for a hectic, urban environment where there was little time to drop out of reality. For seventy-five cents you could have some nitrous oxide transferred from a small metal canister into a balloon and the gas could be inhaled while in the store. A 'high' lasts for one or two minutes.

Nitrous oxide has been appropriately used as an anesthetic during dental surgery. The occasional appropriate use in the dentist's office will not cause serious health problems. However, too much nitrous oxide, taken over an extended period of time, may cause dullness, forgetfulness, difficulty in comprehending, brain damage and even death.

Although there are adults abusing solvents, the major problem is with youth. Why they get involved has been a matter of speculation. A vast number initially try drugs or solvents with the false notion the drug will not cause any harm and that they can be used safely. There is evidence to suggest that once a person gains an appreciation for the health hazards his/her behaviour will change. One former solvent abuser emphatically stated she would never have tried it had she known the dangers.

In summary, the practice of inhalation of volatile products is dangerous. Serious health problems do occur. Some of these problems *cannot* be successfully treated! Life is like a game of chess. We have to watch every move or we may sacrifice our best man! That man is you! **It's better to stop and smell the roses!**

LET'S SEE WHAT YOU'VE LEARNED ABOUT INHALATION ABUSE

What are the health effects of inhalants on the heart and the brain?

The body responds to the inhalation of solvents in four stages. What are some of the health effects which occur in:

Stage 1?

Stage 4?

What are the effects of inhaling nitrites?

What does it mean to develop tolerance to solvent inhalation?

LSD (Acid)

YOU'LL GET BURNED!

LSD (ACID)
You'll Get Burned!

Lysergic acid diethylamide or LSD belongs to a group of drugs classified as the psychedelics. Psychedelics are known for their mind-altering effects. LSD serves as the prototype drug to which all psychedelics may be compared.

On the street, LSD has been referred to as *'Acid', 'John Lennon', 'Northern Lights', 'Blotter', 'California Sunshine', 'Windowpane', 'White Lightning', 'Wedges', 'Yellow Dimples', 'Twenty-Five', 'LSD-25' (because 25 micrograms is enough for a 'hit'), 'Smears', 'Squirrels', 'Purple Barrels', 'Purple Haze',* etc. Probably no other chemical has so many names. Many have suffered severely as a result of using this chemical – *acid does burn!*

> *Murray, a 10-year-old boy, accidentally ate a sugar cube containing 100 micrograms (a microgram is one-thousandth of a gram) of LSD, which his father, a detective, had confiscated from a 'pusher'. Murray had a severe reaction, which included coloured visual distortions, illusions and anxiety. These symptoms became less distressing during the following 3 days, but did not subside. Murray described some of the effects as being similar to having the pain of checkerboards passing through his body. When Murray returned to school a week later he noticed the pages of books and paper wavered and interfered with his reading. He would become upset while looking at the television because he saw movements without the set being on. A lump would form in his throat and he would cling to his father. Some of his days would be completely uneventful, while others would be filled with visual disturbances. One month after the incident he still saw light halos when his eyes were closed. He was hospitalized and made a slow but complete recovery.*

> *Karen, a 22-year-old woman, was married and had a 2-year-old son. Both she and her husband had used drugs, such as LSD, on numerous occasions. She also took amphetamines to help deal with her depression. One day she noticed her son was behaving strangely. He appeared unsteady and stumbled. He was frightened and screamed while looking at the coloured carpet or at the ceiling. He frequently opened his eyes widely and covered his ears with his hands as if to block out unpleasant sounds. Karen suddenly recalled she had two tablets of LSD in her purse and when she went to look for them, she found the purse opened and the tablets missing. The child was taken to a local hospital where the family physician noted symptoms of 'stark terror'. He clung tightly to his mother, screamed at the walls, and would not look at other people or objects. Instead, he appeared to look right through them. He was hyperactive and his heart was racing. The son was transferred to a children's hospital and given necessary medical treatment. The next morning he appeared alert, responsive to commands and appropriate in behaviour. He was discharged the next day and follow-up examination confirmed there were no subsequent reactions to the drug.*

> *Andrew, a 20-year-old college student, became involved with a group of drug-using students. They frequently used marijuana, amphetamine, peyote or mescaline and LSD. His involvement with the group was quite regular. Class attendance became sporadic and his academic performance deteriorated but continued to be of passing quality. One day, Andrew took LSD while with some of his friends. He began to pace in and out of the room. Then without explanation, he disrobed and jumped out a window – to his death!*

The above three cases indicate the serious consequences associated with LSD use. Two of these individuals eventually recovered from the effects of the drug; however, there are others who have not fully recovered and are now institutionalized because the drug actually caused severe brain damage and appeared to have *'fried' their brains*. They are a burden to society because tax dollars are needed to maintain their existence, which in some cases is nothing more than a *mere* existence. If they had not used the drug, in all likelihood, they would be normal functioning individuals enjoying life to its fullest.

LSD was discovered in 1938. In the 1950s, it was used experimentally to treat medical conditions such as schizophrenia and alcoholism. Very quickly this method of treatment was found to be ineffective and fell into medical disfavour. In 1965, the illicit use of LSD reached epidemic proportions because of its reputation as a 'mind-expanding' drug. Since then the drug has routinely been available on the streets, although the supply has varied from time to time. For instance, in the early 1970s, an unfortunate incident in Western Canada substantially decreased the demand. Two teenage boys died from strychnine poisoning. The strychnine was used to 'cut' the LSD. The amount of LSD needed to give a 'hit' is small. In fact, some say 'if you can see the drug, it is too much'. The drug, therefore, has to be in a form that is readily transferable. It is difficult to pass along just a speck of material. A number of the street names suggest ways and means of transportation – for example, blotters or purple barrels. Blotter paper may be impregnated with LSD. Purple barrels are barrel-shaped tablets to which LSD has been added. Unfortunately, for the two boys in Western Canada, the method of transportation was to mix the LSD with sufficient strychnine to ease the transport and sale.

Illicit Use of LSD

LSD is related to a group of compounds known as ergot alkaloids. Alkaloids are basic (non-acidic) substances often obtained from plant sources. The ergot alkaloids are isolated from fungal growth on the plant *Claviceps purpurea*. A number of ergot compounds have been used for certain medical conditions (e.g. migraine headaches). Chemical manipulation of the ergot alkaloids results in the desired illegal product (LSD).

The concentration of LSD, purchased on the street, is between 50 and 300 micrograms. Reactions (illusions) will occur after the ingestion of 25 to 35 micrograms. Because of the small quantity needed, it is not hard to get a number of doses behind a postage stamp (and it has been transported in that manner).

An unusual suit-chewing party!

After LSD is synthesized, it is usually available in the form of a clear, colourless liquid. This liquid is then added to capsules, tablets, powder, other solutions such as coffee, paper (blotter acid, stamps), medications such as aspirin (blue dots), or to gelatin squares (windowpanes). In the New England states, LSD has been reportedly placed on decals designed as temporary tattoos, although some of these reports have turned out to be nothing more than a scare. However, these potential methods of transportation are a cause of concern for children and should serve as a reminder to discuss this possibility with them. There was a report of a user bringing LSD home from Europe camouflaged in a hair tonic bottle. En route, the tonic bottle broke spilling the contents onto the clothes in his suitcase. This did not greatly upset the gentleman. He was still able to hold LSD parties. He simply hung his suit in the living room and had his friends chew on the suit to get their high. A 'suit-chewing' party! What next?

LSD is almost always taken orally. Although it can be smoked, the 'high' is undesirable. Other routes of administration, such as intravenous injection, provide equal effectiveness but have no advantage over oral administration. In fact, this method of administration adds the complication of dirty needles and the health risks associated with their use.

Effects of LSD on the Body

Some of the changes in normal body functioning are due to LSD stimulating both central and peripheral nervous systems. Noticeable are dilated pupils and an increase in alertness. Some authors have subdivided the effects of LSD into three categories: somatic, perceptual and psychic.

The *somatic effects* (those affecting the body) consist of dizziness, upset stomach, nausea, muscle tremors, muscle twitches and anxiety. These effects usually occur within 30 minutes after ingestion.

The *perceptual effects* (those involving sensory stimuli) consist of visual (altered shapes, more vivid colours and difficulty in focussing or blurred vision) and hearing effects (either a sharpened sense of hearing or haphazard hearing). Unlike schizophrenics, LSD users usually recognize that these perceptual effects are drug-related. The trip can usually be completely recalled once the effects of the drug have worn off. The perceptual effects usually occur between 30 to 60 minutes after the drug has been taken.

Some experiences can be rather terrifying.

The *psychic effects* (those affecting the mind) include impaired memory, difficulty in thinking and expression of thoughts, mood alterations, and feelings of tension or a dream-like state. Perhaps the most dangerous psychic effect results from poor judgement, which can lead to fatal accidents. Individuals intoxicated with LSD have received massive burns resulting from long exposure to the sun. Loss of vision has resulted from actually staring at the sun for long periods of time. Others have suffered falls because they felt they had supernatural powers and could fly (see the story of Andrew at the beginning of this chapter). Some have been killed thinking they could stop a moving vehicle. Homicides have also been reported, but it is questionable whether these were a direct result of LSD use. LSD tends to calm the user and, unlike PCP (phencyclidine), makes them less violent.

After 4 to 12 hours, the abuser will usually begin to return to normal, but the effects and the length of time these symptoms are experienced depend, to a great extent, on the dosage of the drug taken.

While the usual effects produced by the drug have been described above, individuals can also be influenced by other factors, which account for variability in experiences described. Mental state and the environment can positively or negatively influence the drug experience.

Adverse Effects and Toxicity of LSD

LSD is a drug that can continue to have an effect long after drug use has been discontinued. The reasons and mechanisms involved are unclear. Panic reactions, also known as a 'bummer' or 'bad trip', are most typical and are probably related to large doses of LSD or to individual variability. Panic reactions, consisting of illusions, feelings of detachment and fear of going insane, are obviously frightening to individuals. In these instances, for some unknown reason, the user does not realize the experience is drug-induced. However, on the positive side, some do realize what is happening and become so frightened that they never touch the drug again. Prolonged psychosis (derangement of personality and loss of contact with reality) may accompany the panic reactions. The outcome of such reactions has been so pronounced that some have committed suicide!

Flashbacks occur less frequently than panic reactions. They are reactions that occur, perhaps without warning, long after the drug has been used. They can occur from 5 to 10 times a day and may occur up to 18 months after drug use. An estimated 5% of LSD users will experience flashbacks. These episodes 'replay' all the effects of the drug including visual changes, distortions in the senses, time and reality. Panic attacks, depression and *deja vu* episodes have also been reported. Although the exact mechanism of flashbacks is unknown, it has been suggested they may be related to abnormalities in brain function similar to epilepsy. Stress, fatigue and the use of other drugs (for example, marijuana and barbiturates) can precipitate flashback reactions.

Plant Sources of Alkaloids Similar to LSD

Earlier in this chapter, it was mentioned that LSD is obtained by chemical manipulation of an alkaloid found in Claviceps purpurea. Morning Glory plants, particularly the seeds, also contain alkaloids related to LSD. It has been known for quite some time that ingestion of Morning Glory seeds can produce similar effects. The seeds are about one-tenth as potent as LSD. Three hundred Heavenly Blue seeds will produce effects equivalent to 200 to 300 micrograms of LSD. Hawaiian Baby Woodrose seeds are 10 times more potent. These seeds were once available for horticultural purposes, but not for human use. As LSD users became more aware of the 'highs' they could obtain from these seeds, their abuse became prevalent and the seeds had to be removed from the legal market.

The following true cases illustrate the effects of Morning Glory seed ingestion.

> *Ken, a 24-year-old man, came from a disturbed home environment. He first learned of the effects from Morning Glory seed ingestion in a newspaper article, which pointed out the dangers of the seeds. After taking the seeds orally and not finding the 'high' entirely satisfactory, he prepared an intravenous injection and administered it to himself. He described the results as being 'dramatic'. Within seconds he was jolted back in his chair. He experienced a feeling of nothingness and became fascinated with his body movements. His head felt detached from his body and he felt he had to move his body slowly to prevent it from falling onto the floor. He also felt very compassionate, loving everyone and everything. About 30 minutes after the injection, he developed an upset stomach, vomiting, diarrhea, chills and blurred vision (which lasted for days).*

He later went into shock and had to be taken to the hospital where he was given supportive medical care. One month later, Ken reported the perceptual distortions returned when he was tired or distracted. He believed he had permanently damaged his brain. Four months later he felt powerfully attracted to the drug. He thought the sensations could be made to return at will, but sometimes recurred against his will. Despite his negative experience, Ken planned to continue using psychedelic drugs.

Ron, a 24-year-old university student, chewed 300 Heavenly Blue seeds and experienced an 'illusion type' experience. He became worried when the effect of the drug did not wear off after 8 hours. In an effort to alleviate the effect he took a sedative but the experience continued for another 24 hours. For the next three weeks, Ron was somewhat exhilarated with the experience, when without warning, his 'illusion type' symptoms recurred. He denied taking any similar drugs and felt as if he could not control his thoughts. He began to experience ringing in his ears and became fearful of going insane. His symptoms would come and go spontaneously. One morning, a week after the recurrence, Ron awakened feeling very upset. He got dressed, drove his car to a nearby hill, and committed suicide by driving down a hill and into a house at 100 miles per hour.

LSD is a devastating drug, as are the related chemicals found in Morning Glory seeds. It is sad to read about the many lives that have been wasted and lost prematurely because of someone selling a 'high'. Because it takes so little of the drug to give a 'hit' one can easily overdose and be 'spaced-out' for a long time. Many LSD users have become so scared or upset with what is happening that they resort to drastic measures, such as what happened to Ron in the case described above. The number of young people institutionalized because of a 'bad trip' is a constant reminder that *LSD* ingestion is dangerous -*YOU CAN GET BURNED!*

LET'S SEE WHAT YOU'VE LEARNED ABOUT LSD

How much LSD is needed to have an effect?

How might LSD be sold?

What are some of the perceptual effects of LSD use?

What are some of the psychic effects of LSD use?

What are flashbacks?

PCP
(Phencyclidine)

AN ANGEL IN BLACK WINGS

PCP (PHENCYCLIDINE)
An Angel In Black Wings

PCP or phencyclidine, also referred to as 'Angel Dust', 'Peace Pill', 'Hog' and 'Horse Tranquilizer', is a dangerous drug. In fact, it is **one of the most dangerous drugs ever to be sold on the streets.** Although it differs in structure and properties to the other psychedelics in that it causes hallucinations or distortions in perception, it is often taken for the purpose of causing 'illusionogenic' effects (mental impressions derived from misinterpretation of actual experiences) and is thus classified as a psychedelic.

A major difference between phencyclidine and the other members of the psychedelic group is the degree of toxicity produced. Severe adverse reactions and fatalities have been reported with PCP. The drug is considered to be extremely dangerous. Only alcoholism, in its final stages, and the continual use of marijuana, due to its fat solubility, have such devastating effects on the brain.

The following cases illustrate the dangers associated with PCP use.

> *Mike, an 18-year-old teenager, was brought to the emergency department a few days after having taken what was supposedly LSD. He was brought in because he was extremely agitated. While in the emergency department his agitation increased, he became paranoid and subsequently leaped out of a window. He was retrieved by security guards and sent home with his mother. Twenty-four hours later, he was brought back because his agitation increased rather than improved. He was then admitted to the psychiatric ward where recovery was realized after twenty-five days of treatment. Only after his recovery was Mike able to recall that the drug he took was not LSD, but PCP.*

> *Gordon, a 24-year-old man, was observed wandering in the hallway of his apartment building. Dressed in a white sheet, he was knocking on all the doors in the hallway, stating he was Jesus Christ and that he was hungry. His wife gestured to others by pointing to her head, indicating he was confused. Two days later both were found dead lying across one another, on top of the bed. Both Gordon and his wife were known to have experimented with marijuana; however, a subsequent investigation revealed that PCP was the drug responsible for their deaths.*

> *Lynn was a 27-year-old woman who had used phencyclidine regularly over a four-year period. One day while planning to go swimming, she smoked a 'crystal joint' (leaf material which could be marijuana, to which PCP has been added) prior to entering the pool. While her boyfriend was changing into his bathing suit, she dove into the pool. Lynn was found a few minutes later dead, at the bottom of the pool. Autopsy revealed no head or neck injuries. The only drug present in her body at the time of death was phencyclidine.*

Although phencyclidine was first discovered in the late 1920s, it wasn't until 1957 before it was realized the chemical had anesthetic properties. As a result, phencyclidine was marketed as a general anesthetic for human use. Unfortunately, physicians soon began to notice that patients, in whom PCP had been used, were experiencing serious adverse effects. The patients, while recovering from surgery, were agitated, disorientated, delirious and experienced visual illusions (a state of being intellectually deceived). Thus, in 1965, medical use of the drug was discontinued. The drug was available for veterinary use, functioning as a suitable anesthetic or tranquilizing agent for animals. The adverse effects seen in humans are not evident in animals.

It is believed the first illegal use of phencyclidine was confined to North America. San Francisco has the dubious honour of being the city where it all started! The illegal use of phencyclidine was initially short-lived because word spread quickly that PCP caused 'bad trips'. Thus, phencyclidine use became virtually absent, at least for a short period of

That inebriated feeling!

time. Unfortunately, the 'bad trips' were soon forgotten and in the 1970s the drug regained its popularity and, once again, was used by many first-time drug abusers for its hopefully pleasurable effects (a lie used by drug dealers to sell the drug). Despite the undesired effects associated with its use, by the mid-1970s PCP use was considered to have reached epidemic proportions.

For street use, PCP is manufactured mainly in illegal laboratories and sold dishonestly as THC (tetrahydrocannabinol, the psychoactive ingredient in marijuana), cannabinol (another marijuana constituent), mescaline, psilocybin (Magic Mushrooms), LSD, amphetamine, cocaine, or by some other name. This deceitful selling technique is an attempt to camouflage what was really being offered to the unsuspecting buyer, probably because of the bad publicity PCP had received in the late 1960s. It is a bit unsettling to find out that in the mid-1970s *only* 3% of the phencyclidine on the streets was actually sold as PCP. Most of the PCP was sold under some other guise so many buyers were not getting the drug they assumed they were buying. Instead they were purchasing a drug (often identified as PCP by laboratory analysis) known to totally devastate the brain. These purchases are referred to as 'burn transactions'. It's not uncommon to be sold something other than what you think you are buying – and some of these transactions are **criminal.** On the other hand, others have purchased what was assumed to be a specific drug only to find they had purchased something which had no effect. An example of such a burn transaction is the individual who bought a capsule filled with Kool-Aid®. A real rip-off! The buyer, in the Kool-Aid® incident, was fortunate because there would be no brain damage, only the experience of psychological frustration from being ripped off! Just because you may trust the individual from whom you make the purchase, remember he or she had to get the drug from someone else, who in turn purchased it from some unknown individual and so on. Burn transactions are very common!

Many drug dealers are trying to make a fast buck. If they can sell you something diluted, or laced with such things as PCP which will give you a fast trip, they will do it. Millions of dollars are exchanged daily by drug dealers!

Since the 1980s, PCP popularity has grown. As a result, phencyclidine is now sold more often as PCP and is not camouflaged by some other name.

Speaking of unpredictable, violent behaviour...

Phencyclidine Administration

Phencyclidine may be taken by swallowing, smoking, snorting, or by injection. Absorption is rapid and the effects may last for hours or days. The duration of effect is determined, to some extent, on the dose. Because PCP is soluble in fat, the body can retain it for weeks and even months after use.

Effects of Phencyclidine

As previously stated, phencyclidine effects may last for an extended period of time, depending on the amount of the drug taken. The effects may be conveniently classified under two general categories, i.e. physical and psychological.

Physically, dizziness, drowsiness, stupor, variable pupil size, blurred vision, tremors, muscle rigidity, increased heart rate, increased blood pressure and increased respiration may be experienced.

Psychological effects include distortion of body image (the person feels as if he has enlarged limbs and a detached head) and an inebriated feeling (like drinking too much). The user could be disoriented and 'out of touch' with reality. Sleeping is not an escape, as dreams become very vivid. As the user begins to lose his or her ability to handle and 'compute' the sensory input, messages going to and from the brain do not result in appropriate responses to such things as sensations of touch, heat, or cold. The user begins to experience a numbing sensation and eventually loses the perception of pain. Remember this drug was used as an anesthetic, so it's not surprising that you do not feel any pain while under the influence of PCP. At this stage, it is very easy for injuries to go unnoticed.

Agitation and hostility are not uncommon. These effects are believed to be related to the individual's make-up, rather than to the direct effects of the drug. High dosages of PCP can result in convulsions, respiratory arrest (cessation of breathing) and death. If coma develops, it may last a few hours or as long as days.

PCP at any dose, but especially at higher doses, may lead to psychotic reactions (mental disorders) which are hard to distinguish from schizophrenia. Like cocaine, PCP interrupts and interferes with the normal functioning of chemicals naturally present in the brain. Normally these chemicals are uniquely kept in balance. The chemicals are necessary for specific functions. When needed they are released from storage sites and attach to receptors, initiating chemical reactions. Any chemical that is not used by the receptors is taken back to the original storage site by a 'reuptake' process. PCP interferes with the functioning of this reuptake process, and thus, excess chemical is sitting around continually bombarding the receptor sites. This upset in the chemical balance is responsible for the abnormal behaviour. Excess dopamine in the brain has been identified as a contributing factor of schizophrenia.

The psychotic effects produced by PCP have resulted in a number of bizarre accidents. The user tends not to fear potentially life-threatening situations. For example, while under the effects of PCP, some have been known to try and stop a train, climb into a polar bear's cave to take pictures, or jump from windows or cliffs. One abuser even pulled out his front teeth with a pair of pliers (no pain felt) and another gouged at his eyes while being questioned by the police. Others have committed homicides and suicides, typically in a violent fashion. More stories could be related, but the point that users may behave irrationally has already been made.

PCP triggers unpredictable and uncontrollable responses from two parts of the brain – the hypothalamus, which controls rage responses and escape reactions, and the cortex, which controls reasoning ability. The result can be an irrational individual who feels cornered and lashes out violently or attempts outrageous acts. Not all individuals who try PCP will experience all of these reactions but it is important to note that *you never know when a bad trip will occur!*

Pleasant effects described by some users have not been the experience of everyone. A good example of the long-lasting detrimental effects of this drug has been aptly portrayed in the film 'Epidemic I'. PCP is undoubtedly one of the most dangerous recreational drugs available. The fact that drug dealers are adding PCP to other drugs is the single best reason to stay away from the drug scene altogether. The street terminology for this drug 'Angel Dust' is quite inappropriate. Angel Dustin, a member of a rock group (sometimes referred to as the PCP Band) is absolutely wrong when he says, "no one would ever commit a violent crime or commit suicide while taking drugs, unless he was going to do it anyway." The alteration in brain chemical balance caused by PCP results in abnormal behaviour and abnormal reactions.

PCP cannot be considered an 'angel' since *angels do not have black wings!*

LET'S SEE WHAT YOU'VE LEARNED ABOUT PHENCYCLIDINE

Some of the effects of PCP use result in irrational behaviour. Why is this?

What is meant by the terminology 'burn transactions'?

What are some of the physical effects of PCP use?

What are some of the psychological effects of PCP use?

OTHER PSYCHEDELICS

THERE ARE NO PLEASANT DREAMS

OTHER PSYCHEDELICS

There Are No Pleasant Dreams

MAGIC MUSHROOMS

In addition to LSD, there are other drugs which may be classified under the heading of psychedelics (compounds which are known for their mind-altering effects). One of these has been referred to as *'Hallucinogenic Fungi'* or, more commonly, *'Magic Mushrooms'*. These so-called Magic Mushrooms contain a substance known as psilocybin. Psilocybin and psilocin are the chemical components of the mushroom responsible for the psychedelic effects. Psilocybin is found in about 40 mushroom species that grow in North America, Europe, Australia and Southeast Asia. The mushroom requires warmth and sunshine for growth, thus the incidence of mushroom abuse proliferates, at least in North America, during the autumn months, i.e. after a warm summer. In other words, the harvest time for mushrooms is the same as for wheat. One newspaper article entitled 'Magic Mushrooms Make Annual Return to City' suggested the mushrooms are most abundant in the fall, making their appearance on the market a seasonal occurrence. Although mushrooms are considered to be used by the lowest economic strata of illicit drug users, the same article went on to describe the arrest of a local man who was attempting to traffic 40 kilograms of the drug, with a total street value estimated at $400,000.

Some of the effects of mushroom ingestion are similar to those described for LSD.

> *Dan, a 25-year-old man with no previous psychiatric history, was a frequent user of marijuana, LSD and mushrooms. On this particular occasion Dan ingested mushrooms. He had not taken any LSD for several days but gathered huge quantities of mushrooms and began eating handfuls of them throughout the day. He also drank*

whiskey and smoked marijuana. He began to feel 'good'. Colours appeared more vivid and he experienced a sense of time loss. Dan estimated he ingested at least 200 mushrooms when he developed a sudden paranoid reaction and threatened three detectives who arrested him. When Dan was released the next day, he described having a disturbed sleep pattern, being irritable, apathetic (could care less) and experienced difficulty concentrating. Dan was treated with tranquilizers and antidepressants for his anxiety and depression. His condition did not seem to improve. This was probably because he continued to ingest more mushrooms (50) on two separate occasions. He declined to be admitted to hospital and was given an increased dosage of antidepressants. Dan took an overdose of the antidepressants and had to be admitted to hospital. Two days later he experienced a flashback, accompanied by visual distortions. He became panicky, aggressive and smashed several windows before attacking the nursing staff. He discharged himself but the local police noticed his disturbed behaviour and he was re-admitted. No improvement was seen after two weeks. Beneficial results were finally obtained by giving Dan four sessions of shock therapy. Dan was discharged after ten weeks in the hospital.

Psilocybin comes in the form of a small mushroom stock, often pulverized into a flaky powder depending on how dry the mushroom has become. The ingestion of between 20 to 30 mushrooms is the usual quantity required for a 'trip' to last between 4 to 6 hours (compare this number of mushrooms with the quantity Dan consumed).

Magic Mushrooms may be eaten, either fresh or dried, or they can be taken by sniffing, smoking or injecting. Injecting plant material is 'loaded' with problems! Much of the material does not dissolve and if injected could cause blood clots. Other components of the mushrooms are foreign to the body. The body has never been exposed to substances like these before and begins to build up antibodies to 'fight them off'. These foreign substances could cause any number of health problems.

Health Effects of Magic Mushroom Use

As indicated previously, a number of the health effects seen with Magic Mushroom or psilocybin use are similar to those of LSD (the reader may wish to refer to the chapter "LSD (Acid)-You'll Get Burned!"). Some of the specific effects of psilocybin, reported by physicians, are best described by Drs. Peden and Pringle, University of Dundee, Department of Pharmacology and Therapeutics. They describe 44 patients, chiefly school children and unemployed youths, seen at the emergency department of their local hospital after the ingestion of 'liberty caps'. Liberty caps are like Magic Mushrooms in that they contain psilocybin.

Most of the young people came to the emergency department because of restlessness, anxiety and a feeling of an impending serious illness. Four of their patients came because they feared they were about to die. On examination in the hospital, all but four of the above patients had dilated pupils. Some of the patients had heart rates of greater than 100 beats per minute (normal rate is between 60 and 80 beats per minute) and diastolic blood pressure of 100 mm of mercury or greater (normal is 80 mm of mercury or less). Other symptoms noted in these patients, although not in all of them, included hyper-reflexes, flushing of the upper trunk of the body, neck, and face, nausea, vomiting, and abdominal pain. Distortions of perception were very common and these distortions were usually visual (i.e. they were seeing things differently than what actually existed). Some of the patients appeared to be hallucinating. Many experienced numbness, prickly, burning sensations of the limbs and face. Two of the young people suffered from ataxia (lack of muscle coordination). In other words, they gave the impression they were drunk or inebriated. Most of the patients were able to leave the emergency department within 1 to 8 hours; however, they were placed in the care of a responsible adult. Eighteen of the patients actually had to be admitted to the hospital but recovered within 12 hours. The effects of the mushroom ingestion were, in this case, short-lived. They obviously had not ingested enough mushrooms.

A Magic Mushroom?

It is apparent that the 'trip' experienced by mushroom ingestion, injection or snorting is not always pleasant. Many of the experiences are upsetting to the individual users. Numerous individuals tell you **there are no pleasant dreams** – a carefree, dream-like state was not experienced.

A note of caution is necessary in concluding a section on mushroom ingestion. Large numbers of young people have been collecting and ingesting mushrooms from various collection spots throughout North America. These collectors are not trained in the identification of mushrooms or toadstools. Accurate identification can only be made by an expert mycologist (a specialist in the study of fungi) or botanist. The ingestion of a poisonous mushroom or toadstool has to occur only once! The outcome is **death!**

MESCALINE

Mescaline is an alkaloid (an alkaloid is a basic chemical substance of plant origin, although some alkaloids are now synthesized in laboratories) found in a species of the *Peyote* cactus known as *Lophophora williamsii*. This plant is a small, fleshy, spineless cactus that grows in arid regions of Mexico and the Southwestern United States, especially along the Rio Grande Valley. Although mescaline is the major alkaloid found in this cactus, there are more than 30 other such compounds. The health effects of the other alkaloids are not clearly defined. We do know, however, that mescaline is the chemical that is responsible for the psychedelic effects.

Mescaline, or peyote, is available on the street as small button-shaped material known as 'peyote buttons'. These buttons are obtained by slicing small circular portions off the cactus and allowing them to dry to increase their potency. The resulting hard brownish buttons or disks maintain their psychedelic activity even on prolonged storage. The buttons may be softened in the mouth, made into a tea or ground and packaged in a capsule to avoid the very bitter taste. A liquid extract of peyote has also been sold on the street as a synthetic or chemically prepared product. Unless an intact peyote button is obtained from the distributor of the drug, it is unlikely the drug purchased is mescaline. Analyses of alleged mescaline street purchases have revealed such things as LSD, PCP, amphetamines, aspirin and even strychnine (rat poison). These examples point out again the uncertainty of purchases made on the street. Some of them are more potent than anticipated and could be dangerous, while others are simply 'rip-offs'!

Peyote was used in Mexico by the Aztecs in religious ceremonies. In the United States, peyote cults began to appear and peyote use in Indian religious ceremonies rapidly became widespread, leading to the formation of the Native American Church in 1918. In this church, peyote-eating was a sacramental rite of communion and members were exempted from prosecution under the Controlled Substances legislation.

Mescaline Health Effects

Approximately 45 milligrams of mescaline is needed to obtain a 'high'. This equates to between 4 and 12 peyote buttons, although the potency of the buttons is impossible to determine. Mescaline is rapidly absorbed and within one-half to one hour, gastrointestinal symptoms such as nausea and vomiting occur. Other symptoms include diarrhea, excessive perspiration, dilation of the pupils, and hyper-reflexes, along with mild increase in heart rate and blood pressure. After the gastrointestinal symptoms begin to resolve, usually within 4 to 6 hours after ingestion, a 'sensory phase' develops similar to that seen with LSD. Sensory phase symptoms include abnormal visual perceptions such as an intensification of colour and geometric imagery, anxiety, emotional upset leading to paranoia and suicidal tendencies.

Other Psychedelics

There is a group of amphetamines that could be appropriately classified under this heading. The reader is asked to refer to the chapter "Amphetamines – 'Speed' Can Kill".

In summary, the psychedelic drugs are those drugs that have the capability of altering perception. Some of these effects may appear pleasant at the time; however, the paranoia, suicidal tendencies and the whole problem of the unknown should make one very uneasy of ever trying these drugs. As with any drug, it is extremely hard to stop the abuse once it is started. The whole scene exemplifies the fact there are **no pleasant dreams!**

LET'S SEE WHAT YOU'VE LEARNED ABOUT THE OTHER PSYCHEDELICS

Why is it dangerous to get involved with mushroom use?

What is the source of mescaline?

What are some of the health effects of mushroom use?

What are some of the health effects of mescaline use?

AMPHETAMINES

'SPEED' CAN KILL

AMPHETAMINES
'Speed' Can Kill

Amphetamines, and a number of drugs chemically related to amphetamines, have surfaced on the streets. One of these derivatives, methamphetamine, has been given the name 'Speed', because of the effects it produces when injected. Amphetamine itself is a simple chemical compound that was developed in the late 1800s. In 1932, amphetamine was marketed as a nasal decongestant, and soon thereafter, its stimulant properties were recognized and amphetamine was used to treat a variety of medical disorders including schizophrenia and morphine addiction. In fact, over the next 10 years, up to 39 medical conditions were being treated with amphetamines. In response to the rising trend with amphetamine use, many pharmaceutical manufacturers began developing chemical derivatives of the original amphetamine molecule with the hope of producing a better medication.

The initial effects of amphetamine use include increased alertness and a lack of feeling tired. Before you say this is just what you need, please read on! Frequently, users feel they are able to 'take on the world' and are better equipped to perform any number of tasks. One amphetamine user felt his ability at sports was greatly enhanced and he could not see any harm in the occasional use of amphetamine. Part of the harm was his conviction and mandatory jail sentence for his drug involvement. This fellow was a young, husky teenager who had so much potential. Unfortunately, drugs were robbing his potential. He would not admit knowledge of the dangers of his drug habit. What a waste of a good life!

> *Rhonda, a 21-year-old female, had been taking amphetamine in large doses over the past six years. The effects of the drug gradually caused insomnia (difficulty in sleeping), weight loss and headaches. Before Rhonda was*

admitted to the hospital she was experiencing thoughts of persecution. She became agitated, anxious, disoriented and developed speech problems. Rhonda was treated and released from hospital only to be admitted to another hospital for similar problems a year later. The difference this time was that Rhonda was not using amphetamine prior to this admission. Even after a whole year her recovery was not complete.

Rick, a 27-year-old pharmacist, was admitted to the hospital almost three years after he started taking amphetamines. The drug had been prescribed by his physician for weakness, fatigue and other symptoms. The initial treatment dose was 18 milligrams. Rick developed tolerance to the initial doses of the drug and began taking 10 times the amount (180 milligrams) in order to achieve the effects he felt on that first dose of 18 milligrams. At these doses, side effects developed that included insomnia, weight loss and irregular heartbeats. Finally, Rick realized he had a problem with the drug and voluntarily entered the hospital. After fighting withdrawal symptoms for 12 days, and several weeks of recovery, Rick was discharged from the hospital.

During World War II, amphetamines were frequently used by military personnel. Following the war, use spread to the streets. In the early 1970s, the use of amphetamine and its related derivatives, which were prepared by reputable pharmaceutical companies, was out of control. There were too many prescriptions being issued for these drugs. At the same time, there was a significant discrepancy between the number of amphetamine drugs produced and the number that were prescribed. It became evident to government departments that these drugs were being distributed illegally through the 'black market'. In an attempt to partially decrease amphetamine use, strict controls were placed on physicians who wished to prescribe them. There were only two conditions for which amphetamines could be prescribed and these conditions had to be verified by a second physician. In addition, a reporting system was put into place, which meant extensive paperwork

Digging out those non-existant worms!

for the physicians. The number of prescriptions for medicinal amphetamines decreased as much as 90% after these controls were implemented.

We have not seen the end of the amphetamine abuse on the street scene. New derivatives of amphetamine were, and are, being developed in underground laboratories. These derivatives were probably the first so-called 'designer drugs'. Forensic laboratories have identified many of these newly designed drugs and, as a result, the drugs are now appropriately covered within the laws of our countries.

Patterns of Addiction

Amphetamine abuse differs from cocaine abuse in that its duration of effect is slower to develop and lasts longer than cocaine. Because cocaine acts so quickly, the effect or 'high' is also shorter. An amphetamine 'high' may last for hours. Amphetamine abuse usually begins with occasional use of relatively small dosages, but dependence soon takes hold, and these small dosages are taken with increased frequency. As use continues, the individual may find the need for sedatives, such as alcohol or barbiturates, to relax or sleep. The pattern of stimulant-depressant-stimulant abuse is dangerous. Individuals have died after this type of drug cycle. One university student took a stimulant to stay awake in order to study but needed a depressant to fall asleep. He became sick during the night but did not sufficiently arouse to realize what was happening. He choked to death on his own vomit.

Continued use of orally administered amphetamines often leads to intravenous use. Sometimes many repeated injections, called a 'run', are made to obtain a rush or 'orgasmic' reaction and a state of mental alertness and euphoria. If this type of abuse continues for several days, the person can become paranoid and may experience delusions of bugs crawling on the skin. This condition is known as 'formication'. Physicians have had to treat patients who have tried to dig at these non-existent bugs or worms. Knives or other sharp objects have been used to cut the skin in an attempt to relieve the sensation. This effect is actually due to stimulation of the nerve endings, rather than bugs. During this paranoid stage, individuals may also behave in a bizarre, violent manner. It is not uncommon for them to commit homicides, smash windows, or destroy valuable property.

It is impossible for abusers to maintain this continual state of excitation. They eventually collapse from exhaustion and fatigue. The addict then sleeps for days. During this time the individual may experience severe depression which is only relieved by injecting the drug again.

The 'Street' Amphetamines

There are 30 or more different amphetamines available on the street. A number of these amphetamines have been labelled with identifying initials. They may be described as an 'alphabet soup'. Examples include, MDA (methylenedioxyamphetamine), MDMA (3,4-methylene-dioxymethamphetamine, also known as Ecstasy), and DOM or STP (dimethoxy-methylamphetamine). These amphetamines are synthesized in illegal laboratories, known in drug culture terminology as 'clandestine' laboratories.

Methylenedioxyamphetamine (MDA)

Medical reports emphasize the fact that these drugs are **not** just mildly toxic, but **can** cause death!

> *Tom, a 32-year-old man, was admitted to the hospital in a comatose state. History from his friend was vague, but Tom was a known drug user. He had been at a party where drugs were being used and was later found in the bedroom totally unresponsive. When Tom was brought to the hospital he had high blood pressure, elevated pulse and respiration rate, and a high body temperature. His body was very rigid and his eyes were abnormal. He had what is referred to as 'doll's eyes'. The physicians responded to Tom's condition with vigorous treatment in an attempt to improve his medical condition. Tom's condition initially stabilized after two seizures, but then he began to suffer from diarrhea and hemorrhaging from the nose. His condition continued to deteriorate. He was taken to the operating room but died shortly afterward from repeated cardiac arrests. Blood and urine analyses were positive for methylenedioxyamphetamine.*

> *Mark, a 22-year-old Caucasian male, had been using amphetamines, barbiturates and various psychedelics for one year. One night, he and five other friends each took a single capsule containing approximately 500 milligrams (one-half gram) of MDA. This was Mark's first experience with the drug. After 15 minutes he had an epileptic-like seizure and lost consciousness. He was rushed to the emergency department by ambulance. Twenty-four hours after the incident, Mark regained normal mental status with no evidence of psychotic after-effects. He was discharged from the hospital 3 days later having had quite a scare.*

> *Marcus, a 25-year-old male, had a long history of oral and intravenous drug abuse. He had previously taken MDA several times but only in small doses. He accompanied his friend Mark, the 22-year-old described in the above scenario, to the hospital and was not ill at the time. However, shortly after arriving at the emergency department with Mark, Marcus became hyper-alert and talkative. He did not appear to develop seizures or breathing problems. He was discharged but returned to the emergency department the next night complaining of 'seeing things' (visual hallucinations) even though he had not taken any drugs after being discharged. The effects persisted over the next 24 hours.*

MDA or methylenedioxyamphetamine has the reputation of providing a 'good trip' or a 'tranquil psychedelic experience', earning the drug the street name 'love drug'. This type of love is one that you can do without!

Methylenedioxymethamphetamine (MDMA, Ecstasy)

For a full discussion of this amphetamine, please refer to the chapter "Ecstasy – Nothing to 'Rave' About".

Dimethoxymethylamphetamine (DOM OR STP)

Dimethoxymethylamphetamine was originally given the name DOM to coincide with the major chemical substituents attached to the amphetamine molecule (dimethoxymethyl). STP, a chemical you might be most familiar as an additive for motor oil, also became a name for this amphetamine derivative indicating 'serenity, tranquillity and peace'. The effects of this amphetamine are similar to mescaline (see chapter on "Other Psychedelics – There Are No Pleasant Dreams"), except that DOM or STP is 40 to 50 times more potent. DOM usage is associated with a high incidence of panic reactions.

Methamphetamine (Speed)

Methamphetamine, the methyl derivative of amphetamine, is commonly referred to as 'Speed'. This drug is generally taken by injection, producing stimulant effects similar to that seen with amphetamine itself. Speed can kill and has! The effects of Speed are not unlike the amphetamines described above.

Smokable Methamphetamine (Ice)

Amy, an attractive 25-year-old woman, was hooked on Ice after the first hit. Smoking methamphetamine gave her the energy she needed to work all day, keep her house spotless and socialise every evening. Things were great at first, even her and her boyfriend got along better when they were high. Then she started hearing voices; they were talking about her and about her boyfriend. Strangers were talking about how her boyfriend was seeing other women. She was becoming more and more paranoid. She started believing that people wanted to break into her house and kill her. One day at work Amy broke down. Her boss was sympathetic and helped her get into a drug treatment centre. Amy has been clean ever since.

In late 1988 and early 1989, Hawaii became known as the trendsetter for **'Crystal Meth' abuse.** In fact, the Star Bulletin and

There are enough amphetamines to make alphabet soup.

Honolulu Advertiser stated there was concern nationwide that smokable Crystal Meth meant the beginning of a new epidemic. They further reported, "the Crystal Meth was a cunning drug, manoeuvring itself from a quick smoke with an energized, long-lasting high to something akin to demonic possession." Crystal Meth also became directly or indirectly linked to one-third of the murders in Oahu alone (Honolulu Advertiser – August 4, 1990). There were concerns that the well-publicized dangers of crack meant some abusers were switching to crystals of methamphetamine thinking it was a safer drug. But they were wrong! The crystals, also called 'Ice', are the amphetamine-equivalent to crack cocaine, **but the effects last 10 times longer than crack!** Ice is heated in the bowl of a pipe and the vapours are inhaled. The effects are almost instantaneous – like injecting the drug without a needle! The 'high' lasts much longer than crack. The higher and longer the 'high', the more severe the depression once the effect of the drug wears off. Some cannot cope with the depression and know it can be relieved quickly by smoking more Ice. This begins the vicious circle leading to addiction.

Toxic effects of Ice are similar to those caused by oral or injectable forms of methamphetamine but may occur earlier. These include paranoia (similar to schizophrenia), hallucinations (that often include the delusion of bugs crawling over the body), and hearing voices that can last for some time after the drug has been discontinued. One abuser describes the voices as if there is no privacy – "it feels like people are reading your mind." No wonder abusers begin to freak out! Patients have also suffered from strokes as a result of overuse of the drug. There have been deaths from simply smoking the drug – one patient developed extensive spasms of the veins, which precipitated a heart attack, shock and death. Others have become quite obsessive in their behaviour – one young woman became obsessed with keeping her home clean; she even began to scrub the corners of the floor with a toothbrush.

Hawaii was considered to be leading the nation (United States) in the use of crystal methamphetamine partially because the drug was coming from Asia. Although the drug has been detected in Canada, its use is not as extensive as that reported in the United States. This does not mean we should be complacent. The drug is around, available and is probably one of the most addicting drugs ever to reach the streets of our country.

114

Prescribed Amphetamines

There are amphetamine derivatives that may be prescribed by physicians. These drugs are perfectly safe to take in their prescribed dosages. Abuse potential is always there, but an awareness of the potential dangers may prevent the possibility of being caught up in a 'Speed' trap (or with any of the other addictive amphetamine derivatives). The truth is, names like 'Speed', 'love drug', 'STP', and 'Ecstasy' are inappropriate, false designations. They imply that the effects they are supposed to produce are desirable, but one can clearly see that they are, in fact, too good to be true and should immediately alert you of a **'danger signal'**.

LET'S SEE WHAT YOU'VE LEARNED ABOUT AMPHETAMINES

What is Speed?

What is Ice?

What comparisons can be made between crack and Ice?

What are some of the health effects of amphetamine drugs?

What are some names of amphetamine drugs (that are the reason for referring to them as alphabet soup)?

ECSTASY

NOTHING TO 'RAVE' ABOUT

ECSTASY

Nothing To 'Rave' About

A February 2000 newspaper article stated: "The illicit international drug trade has been updated for the 21st century. Today's version involves the designer drug Ecstasy, and drug experts say it is being manufactured in 'underground' laboratories in the Netherlands and Belgium. European organized crime is once again feeding the exploding North American market for the euphoria-inducing, mind-altering chemical. It is using tourist flights from countries not traditionally known as drug sources (France, Germany and Spain) to illegally smuggle Ecstasy into Toronto, Miami, Los Angeles and New York. Drug investigators say use of Ecstasy is widespread in virtually every major city in North America. The drug is being sold by hundreds of dealers in coffee shops, hamburger joints and shopping malls and its use is rampant in most after-hour clubs and all-night rave parties. The brightly coloured pills, sold for $20 to $40 each, cost between 50 cents and $3.00 to make. In 1997, 400,000 doses were seized in the United States, but in 1999 they seized nearly 3 million doses. Alarmingly, in a recent four-month period more than 3 million doses were seized – a gigantic problem!" Teenagers are being arrested on arrival at international airports after body searches reveal Ecstasy. Two teenagers were busted in Toronto with more than 34,000 pills, worth an estimated $1.2 million on the street.

Ecstasy is one street name for the chemical MDMA (3,4-methylenedioxymethamphetamine). This drug was initially synthesized in 1912, to be marketed as an appetite suppressant, but it never became commercially successful. It resurfaced in the 1950s as a psychotherapeutic agent for the treatment of individuals with psychological problems, but in 1985 it was classified as a restricted drug because of its toxic effects. In the mid-1980s it re-emerged as a recreational drug used primarily among college students and other young adults. It has become popular with adolescents at dance halls

118

known as 'raves' and sold as 'Ecstasy', 'XTC', 'Adam', and 'E'. The widespread use of Ecstasy by teenagers can be traced to Britain. An estimated 20,000 to 30,000 young people were going to raves every weekend. 'Ravers' dance vigorously and continuously all night, to loud, repetitive, electronic rock music. Ravers engage in vigorous marathon group dancing with expensive laser light displays illuminating the darkened hall. Someone has penned lyrics which explain some of the desired outcomes of the rave: *'this is harmony; what you need to live; everybody's sympathizing, everybody's temperature's rising; lifting me into the heavens in a state of ecstasy; such a good feeling is where I want to be, such a good feeling, in total ecstasy'*. Unfortunately, it is not total ecstasy for some.

> *A coroner's inquest will examine the popular drug, Ecstasy, and the local party scene when it probes the death of 21-year-old Bob, a local university business student who died after ingesting Ecstasy at a rave attended by 3,500 people in an underground parking garage.*

> *Shots rang out at 4:30 a.m. outside a local nightclub. Police say two men refused to allow a bouncer to do a body search and, when asked to leave, started shooting. The all-night rave and dance club, which opens about 10 p.m. and closes as late as 9 a.m., was packed with a few hundred people. It was dark with disco lights flashing. Everyone was dancing, screaming and having a good time. Police say drugs like Ecstasy and LSD are common among patrons at these clubs. When investigators arrived, drugs were dumped on the two dance floors.*

> *Marcia, a 21-year-old woman, experienced pain after ingestion of only one Ecstasy tablet. After being admitted to the hospital, a CT scan and a magnetic resonance (MRI) examination were done. These procedures revealed a left cerebral (brain) hemorrhage. Marcia only partially recovered her neurological functions after one year.*

119

Ecstasy (MDMA) – An Entactogen

Ecstasy was initially thought to be a safe chemical by recreational users and by a few psychotherapists. Some of the effects of the drug on the body are different from other stimulants and hallucinogens and have resulted in Ecstasy being classified as an 'entactogen', that is, it produces enhanced empathy (ability to intellectually and emotionally sense the emotions, feelings, and reactions that another person is experiencing and to effectively communicate that understanding to the individual), introspection (looking within; contemplating one's own mental processes), communication, and induces positive mood states, and feelings of intimacy and tranquility.

Health Effects of Ecstasy

Many of the risks users face with MDMA are similar to those found with the use of amphetamines and cocaine. They are typically psychological and physical effects.

Psychological difficulties, including confusion, depression, sleep problems, drug craving, severe anxiety, paranoia, and delusions. These effects have been reported to occur during and sometimes weeks after taking the drug. Psychotic episodes, mental and behavioural disorders have also been reported.

Physical symptoms include muscle tension, involuntary teeth clenching, nausea, blurred vision, dilated pupils, rapid eye movement, faintness, and chills or sweating. Increased body temperature has been noted on many occasions – sometimes referred to as 'Saturday night fever'. One study looked at the dental effects in Ecstasy users and found that 60% of those in the study wore through their enamel into the underlying dentine. Tooth-grinding is common and even continues for hours after taking the chemical.

Increases in heart rate and blood pressure are a special risk for people with circulatory or heart disease. Blood pressure can increase significantly and the heart rate increases in controlled studies by as much as 30 beats per minute.

Recent research findings link Ecstasy use to long-term damage in those parts of the brain critical to thought and memory processes. It is thought that the drug causes damage to the neurons (the functional unit of the nervous system) that use the chemical serotonin to communicate to other neurons. MDMA is neurotoxic to the brain and behavioural data

Beware of street drug contamination.

suggests that the brain injury is associated with subtle, but significant, cognitive (the mental activities associated with thinking, learning and memory) deficits. Users have difficulty with tasks requiring arithmetic calculations, complex attention and incidental learning, and short-term memory. Evidence from both animal and human studies suggests that repeated administration of Ecstasy produces lasting decreases in serotonin activity which have effects on learning and memory.

There is evidence that users who develop an acne-like rash after using MDMA may be risking severe side effects, including liver damage, if they continue to use the drug.

> *Susan, an 18-year-old female, regularly used Ecstasy over a two-month period. Within 2 days after accepting a 'hit' of the substance at a party, she was admitted to the hospital because of vomiting, lethargy (almost to a state of unconsciousness), abdominal pain, stool discolouration, jaundice and darkened urine. On day 7 she developed major liver failure. This type of failure has life-threatening complications so it had to be quickly handled by performing a liver transplant. Within 3 days after the transplant, Susan made a full recovery and was released from the hospital 6 weeks later.*

Ecstasy and Neurodegeneration

Several researchers have reported that the first Ecstasy tablet taken appears to yield the best 'experience'. Subsequent ingestion of the chemical produces a decline in the desired effects and side effects increase. Needing more of the drug to give the original effect is not uncommon, but the reason for this phenomenon with Ecstasy is different than for some of the other drugs. It is not development of a tolerance to the drug; rather, it appears to be due to neurotoxicity (damage to the nervous system). In fact, some Internet newsgroups that promote the use of Ecstasy are now debating, not whether it causes nerve cell damage, but whether the result is damaging or of no concern. Obviously they acknowledge that it is damaging since their general advice is that "more than one tablet once a month is an overdose".

Summary

It seems logical that easy availability, affordability, the perception of safety, peer acceptance and encouragement to try Ecstasy will lead to increased misadventure with this drug. MDMA has been implicated with a number of serious health effects. While there have been a number of deaths, there have been more reports of serious health consequences including brain damage – with long lasting, possibly permanent effects. There is also the possibility of ingestion of other drugs that may look like Ecstasy which are also associated with their own set of serious health consequences. One such example is 'herbal ecstasy' which has been reported to contain ephedrine or gamma hydroxybutyrate (GHB). Analyses have shown that Ecstasy tablets contain a range of ingredients with widely varying concentrations. Concentrations may vary in strength by as much as seventy-fold. Some tablets contain neither Ecstasy nor related compounds. With all the serious consequences associated with Ecstasy use, one cannot seriously conclude that Ecstasy is still something to 'rave' about?

LET'S SEE WHAT YOU'VE LEARNED ABOUT ECSTASY

Why is Ecstasy referred to as an entactogen?

What are the effects of Ecstasy on the brain?

What are the effects of Ecstasy on the teeth?

Why might an acne-like rash indicate serious toxicity?

PARTY DRUGS

A 'DATE' YOU WOULD RATHER MISS

PARTY DRUGS
A 'Date' You Would Rather Miss

One usually thinks of alcohol and marijuana as the party drugs of the century. While these drugs are being used/abused to a greater extent than at the beginning of the 1990s, other substances deserve highlighting since their use has become prevalent. They are the 'date rape' drugs and are 'dates' you would rather miss. In fact, the alarming and recent rise in use of these drugs has resulted in the National Institute on Drug Abuse to initiate a broad-based public initiative to inform and educate teens, young adults, parents and communities about their dangers.

Three of these substances, **Rohypnol, GHB (gamma-hydroxybutyrate) and ketamine, are central nervous system** depressants and have been known to be part of the party drug scene, including raves. These drugs may be added to beverages without detection since they odourless, tasteless, colourless and quickly dissolve when added to the drink. While they have the distinction of being known as the **'date rape'** drugs, they have also been used for other purposes.

Rohypnol

The following Rohypnol cases illustrate the potency of the drug:

> *Connie thought she was so lucky to meet such a charming fellow at her first university party. Joe had offered her a ride home and suggested they get a drink 'to go'. When he returned he offered Connie a plastic cup filled with beer and the two headed for the door. They talked as they drove. Joe refused to drink while he drove, a fact that made him even more appealing to Connie. They pulled up in front of Connie's house. She complained she was sleepy and*

> *dropped her house keys several times. Joe opened the front door and helped Connie into the house and then told her that he'd put her to bed since her roommates were not home. Connie remembers nothing after that. Early the next morning Connie woke feeling shaky and sore. Stumbling out of bed she realized that she was half-naked and bruised. She had been raped. Crying, she phoned the number Joe had given her only to find that Joe did not live there. She then realized she did not even know Joe's last name.*

> *Tom stopped for a drink at a bar one evening. About 20 minutes later he felt so sleepy he had trouble staying awake and sitting upright. Hours later, he woke up in an alley. He was bruised, bleeding and his clothes were torn. Tom's wallet was also gone. It appeared that when he fell asleep he was taken outside, beaten and robbed.*

These two cases describe what can happen if someone unknowingly ingests Rohypnol. Joe had slipped a white Rohypnol pill into Connie's beer. She did not suspect anything since the pill dissolves so quickly. Someone had also done the same to Tom's drink and then dragged him outdoors. These are only examples of assaults reported throughout the country as a result of Rohypnol use. It is not only young people who have taken advantage of the opposite sex. A recent television news story showed a husband going to jail for 20 years because he used the drug to get even with his wife (he raped her). Kurt Cobain fell into a coma after taking the small powerful pill along with champagne. He was revived by pumping his stomach but unfortunately died a short while later from an overdose of drugs.

Rohypnol is known on the street as 'roofies', the 'forget-me pill', the 'drop drug', 'roachies', 'wolfies', 'roach', 'rope', and of course, the 'date rape' drug. Rohypnol is the trade name for flunitrazepam, a drug which shares the same chemical classification as Valium® – but flunitrazepam is 10 times stronger. Flunitrazepam was initially developed for the treatment of severe insomnia. Today, much of the drug is imported from Mexico and Columbia, since the drug is illegal in the United States. At $1 to $5 a pill it has become popular with teenagers who like to combine it with alcohol for a 'quick punch-drunk hit'. The 'lunch money high' has become part of the gang culture and the rave scene. When mixed with alcohol it can incapacitate a person and prevent them from resisting sexual advances. Death may also result when the drug is taken with alcohol and/or other depressants.

Health Effects Of Rohypnol

The sedating (depressant) effects begin within 15 to 30 minutes after taking the drug, peaks within 2 hours and may last for up to 8 hours or more. A decrease in blood pressure, memory impairment, drowsiness, vision problems, dizziness, confusion, nausea, and difficulty in being able to urinate have been experienced by some users. When taken for an extended period of time, a user can become physically dependent to the drug and when one tries to stop using the drug, they develop withdrawal symptoms such as headache, muscle pain, tension, anxiety, confusion, restlessness, irritability, convulsions, and in some cases, shock and collapse.

Some hallucinate as a result of using Rohypnol and can become aggressive and act out in a rage. Unfortunately, there is no recollection of what you did while under the influence of 'roofies'. One person describes it as, "You take it and black out. The next day people tell you what you did and you're like, 'Wha-a-a-a-t?'"

To protect yourself from unknowingly taking this drug, watch what you drink at parties and on dates. Don't accept a drink from a stranger (this includes coffee, soft drinks) and refuse drinks that are in an open container. Do not leave your drink sitting while you leave the room. Take it with you. You cannot be too cautious with drugs like Rohypnol around.

GHB (Gamma-Hydroxybutyrate)

Some common street names for this drug include 'liquid ecstasy', 'scoop', 'somatomax', 'grievous bodily harm', 'Georgia Home Boy' (because it was one of the most popular drugs manufactured in Atlanta), and 'G'.

Gamma-hydroxybutyrate is found naturally in the central nervous system, kidney, heart and muscle and may play a role in the transmission of impulses within these body organs. It was synthesized in the 1960s as a sedative and as an intravenous anesthetic for use in children but soon fell into disfavor due to its side effects. Since 1990,

GHB has been abused for its euphoric, sedative and anabolic (body-building) effects. GHB purchased on the street is undoubtedly from underground laboratories since it has been banned for sale since 1992 in the United States.

> *Bob, a 70-kg white male, presented to a clinic where he was diagnosed as being dependent on Speed and abusing a number of benzodiazepines. He also admitted daily use (once or twice per day) of GHB for the past 2 years. He took the drug for its euphoric effects and to handle the withdrawal effects of Speed. On one occasion he ingested 15 grams of GHB. He vomited and could not be aroused for 3 hours. He also lost control of his bladder and bowels. Fortunately, he discontinued the use of GHB and did not suffer any further ill effects.*

> *Fred's GHB use resulted in him losing consciousness while he was in charge of looking after his children. This scared him and he was determined to stop using the drug. However, when he stopped, he began to suffer from some profound withdrawal effects including muscle cramps, anxiety and inability to sleep. These symptoms peaked in three days and lessened within one week, except for an additional week of feeling 'drained'. He went back to the health food store and found that GHB was no longer available so he began to buy it from underground sources and in no time was taking the same dose as the dose which originally caused him to lose consciousness. He also began mixing GHB with alcohol and, as a result of a severe relapse, re-entered inpatient treatment. Since detoxification he has not used alcohol, GHB or other mood-altering drugs.*

> *Grace was a regular participant in rave clubs where she took 3 Ecstasy tablets. She says she did not have any adverse effects from this until one evening she took GHB in combination with her usual dosage of Ecstasy. She became agitated and delusional, requiring hospitalization and treatment. After 2 days of hospitalization and medication, she stabilized and suffered no long-term effects. The combination of Ecstasy and GHB had produced a toxic psychosis.*

Health Effects of GHB

GHB is commonly sold as a clear, salty liquid in a bottle similar in size to that of typewriter correction fluid. The usual dose is one or two capfuls. Adverse effect include dizziness, nausea, vomiting, weakness, seizures, loss of peripheral vision, confusion, agitation, hallucinations, slowing of the heart, decreased respiration, unconsciousness and coma. Respiratory arrest reportedly occurred in a male who had several beers and a small amount of GHB. He had to have a tube inserted down his throat so he could be mechanically ventilated. Luckily, he did recover.

It is clear GHB has similar effects to that of Rohypnol. Sexual assault cases have also been reported as a result of this drug.

Ketamine

This anesthetic substance, commonly known as 'Special K', 'Cat' (presumably from ketamine's use as a veterinary anesthetic), or erroneously as 'Vitamin K' and 'Valium', is similar in action to PCP and LSD, although it is less potent. The drug, used for veterinary anesthetic properties, has often been reported as being stolen from their supply sources. It sells for about $20 a dose.

When abused, ketamine, depending upon the dose that is taken, produces a state of dreamy intoxication, often sometimes described as an 'out-of-body' experience, delirium accompanied by inability to move, an inability to feel pain, or amnesia. Deaths have also been associated with ketamine use as a result of the potentially fatal respiratory effects.

Ketamine, a white powder, has sometimes been used as a substitute for cocaine (by snorting). This seems rather strange since cocaine gives you a 'high' while ketamine depresses the central nervous system. It has also been used as a liquid applied to marijuana or tobacco products. Although use of ketamine to facilitate rape has not been reported in great numbers, it has similar potential as does Rohypnol and GHB. It is capable of producing amnesia and impaired motor function, and may be found as an additive to marijuana or tobacco products.

Other Party or Club Drugs

The other drugs which could quite appropriately be discussed in this section include MDMA (Ecstasy, X, XTC, Adam), methamphetamine (Meth, Speed, Ice, Glass, Crystal, Crank) and LSD

130

(Acid, Blotter, Cubes, Dots, L, Sugar). The reader is referred to the specific chapters on Ecstasy, amphetamines, and LSD for more detail. Briefly, for completion of this chapter, **MDMA or Ecstasy** is a stimulant similar to methamphetamine and is usually taken orally as a tablet. It causes increased heart rate and blood pressure, and may lead to an elevation of body temperature that causes kidney and cardiovascular failure. When combined with alcohol, MDMA can be extremely dangerous, sometimes fatal. Chronic abuse may produce long-lasting neurotoxic effects on the brain. **Methamphetamine** is an odourless white crystalline powder, which is a highly addictive stimulant that can be snorted, smoked, injected, or taken orally. The drug produces increased levels of activity, excited speech and decreased appetite. This drug is a neurotoxin associated with long-lasting effects on the dopamine transporter system (a very important brain chemical), as well as other health effects including aggression, violence, memory loss, psychotic behaviour, and cardiac damage. **LSD** is a powerful hallucinogen that is taken orally, usually on squares of blotter paper, sugar cubes, or pills that have absorbed the liquid drug. The drug produces profound abnormalities in sensory perception, including distortions of sound and sight, and emotional effects that create rapid mood swings ranging from intense fear to euphoria.

LET'S SEE WHAT YOU'VE LEARNED ABOUT PARTY DRUGS

What are the names of the party drugs?

What are some of the toxic effects of flunitrazepam?

What are some of the toxic effects of GHB?

Is 'Special K' really special?

What precautions should you take when attending a party?

DESIGNER DRUGS

AN ENGINEERING NIGHTMARE

DESIGNER DRUGS
An Engineering Nightmare

A National Federation of Parents for Drug-Free Youth (NFP) newsletter contained an article, which opened with the following statement, "Their formulas can be found in almost any university chemistry laboratory. They can be made in any undetectable bathroom-size laboratory, beyond the reach of customs officers and eradication programs. One lab can produce the world's demand for them without harvesting a single opium poppy. They are known on the street as 'China White', 'Persian White', and 'Mexican Brown'. What are they? They represent more recent developments in the evolution of mind-altering drugs and are marketed using exotic names ('Eve', 'Ecstasy') – **'designer drugs'**."

Chemists, often amateurs lured by money, manipulate the chemical structures of powerful, regulated drugs to create new drugs, supposedly falling outside federal, provincial or state regulations and jurisdictions. The proliferation of these substance analogues is phenomenal. These so-called 'new drugs' are quickly made and distributed to couriers, who then sell them to eager, unsuspecting individuals who crave a 'high'. They may be told the drug is a first-class, potent, synthetic heroin, or similar type drug. Unfortunately, these 'new drugs' have not been tested for side effects on humans. In fact, they have never been tested on animals! Any new drug developed by a pharmaceutical company must go through years of testing and millions of dollars in research funds before it is considered safe for use as a medication. This means 10 to 20 years of development before being approved for human consumption and can cost in excess of $100 million. It is interesting to note that many potential life-saving drugs, developed by pharmaceutical companies, never make it to market. Some unexpected reactions appear during preliminary testing and they have to be scrapped. Designer drug chemists do not have many failures – at least from their perspective! Hard to believe?

134

Designer drugs have created nightmares for a number of innocent people.

> *Todd, a pre-school child, walked into his parents' bedroom to wake them. They did not respond to his pleas. Why not? Because they were dead! They had overdosed on a 'new heroin type of drug' (a designer drug).*

> *Carl, a previously healthy 25-year-old man, was admitted to the hospital in an immobile, mute state. His girlfriend stated that over the past eight days he had gradually become withdrawn and had stopped talking and eating. He had a long history of drug abuse. No improvement was observed after an eleven-month treatment period in a psychiatric facility. When referred for neurological assessment, the physician noticed he walked with a stooped, shuffling gait, drooled excessively, spoke in a monosyllabic whisper and required assistance to feed himself. A diagnosis of severe Parkinsonism, of unknown cause, was made. There was no family history of Parkinsonism, yet when treated with anti-Parkinson's drugs, he responded dramatically. He was ecstatic! For the first time in a year he was able to speak clearly and to feed himself. He said it was like 'getting out of a cage'. He described snorting a home-made drug daily for seven days before his illness. He had made and taken the compound many times previously without mishap, but something went wrong with the experiment in the batch associated with his illness. Unfortunately, while attending a party on a wharf 20 months after his original illness, Carl fell into the ocean unnoticed and drowned.*

Designer drugs are not new. In the late 1960s, laboratories produced LSD and amphetamine derivatives. The late 1970s and early 1980s brought the potent derivatives of narcotics and other dangerous drugs – an alarming situation. A newly synthesized drug just becomes identified and controlled by law before another appears, which in turn has to be identified and controlled. A real snowball effect! Government officials have had to deal with federal statutes to close the loopholes. In 1986, the Controlled Substance Analogue Enforcement Law was passed

Preparation of a Designer Drug.

in the United States to act as an all-encompassing blanket. This outlaws any compound that has a stimulant, depressant or hallucinogenic effect on the central nervous system similar to, or greater than, an already controlled substance, or which is claimed to possess these attributes by a seller. Terms of imprisonment of up to 15 years and a fine of up to $250,000 for violations involving controlled substance analogues can be imposed. The lead by the United States resulted in the development of legislation to bring Canadian laws into closer harmony.

Designer Drugs Related to Amphetamine

Amphetamine can only be obtained by prescription since it is considered a controlled substance. However, by altering the structure slightly, drug pushers assumed they would avoid getting caught. Thus, a number of designer drugs were manufactured including methylenedioxy-amphetamine (MDA), methylenedioxyethylamphetamine (MDE, Eve), methylenedioxy-methamphetamine (MDMA, Ecstasy), 2,5-dimethoxy-4-methylamphetamine (STP, DOM), trimethoxyamphetamine (TMA), paramethoxyamphetamine (PMA) and others. These analogues were subsequently controlled by legislation. In the 1970s, derivatives of PCP and methaqualone (another so-called 'love drug', more commonly referred to as 'Quaaludes') were discovered, identified and subsequently controlled. In 1982, another derivative of amphetamine, N-ethylamphetamine, became controlled.

Designer Drugs Related to Fentanyl

The 1980s brought a new group of substances – narcotic analogues. Chemical variations of the parent compounds fentanyl (Sublimaze®, Innovar®) and meperidine (Demerol®) were synthesized. Fentanyl is a potent narcotic, which, in humans, is about 100 times as strong as morphine. It is used for anesthesia during surgery. Some of the analogues to this narcotic have resulted in the production of even more potent substances – so potent, in fact, that 1.0 gram is sufficient material for 50,000 doses. Other derivatives are believed to be 1000 to 2000 times more potent than heroin. Fentanyl analogues have been sold on the street as heroin, synthetic heroin, or China White. These analogues have resulted in deaths from overdosage. Other unexplained deaths may have been due to China White overdose but have gone undetected since only minute quantities of the drug are required to depress the respiratory (breathing) centre of the brain. For example, one death in California was obviously due to an overdose of a drug having similar properties to the narcotics. Initial examination of the victim's bodily fluids revealed nothing. A powder found in the possession of the deceased was analysed and revealed the presence of lactose (a sugar-like substance) and nothing more. Subsequent analysis, using more sophisticated instrumentation, revealed the presence of an unfamiliar product. The substance was not identified until another sudden death became the subject of a laboratory investigation. It took nearly a month to come up with the answer. These types of cases are frustrating because a devastating drug can 'get out of hand' before the cause and identity is determined. However, when compounds are not available for as standards for comparison purposes, many painstaking hours by dedicated scientists are needed before an answer is obtained. Solving the puzzle is particularly challenging when the lives of humans are at stake.

> *Paramedics were alerted to a possible drug overdose by an anonymous telephone call. Upon arriving at the scene, the paramedics found John, a 28-year-old male, with respiratory paralysis. He was taken to a hospital where he was pronounced dead on arrival. An investigation verified that John had a history of drug and alcohol abuse. External examination of the deceased revealed a well-developed male with a lesion on his left forearm consisting of yellowed tissue and needle punctures. Internal examination showed some irregularities, but subsequent toxicological analyses could not support the suspicion of alcohol or any other volatile components in the blood. Furthermore, blood analyses did not indicate the presence of sedative/hypnotics (sleeping pills), barbiturates (e.g. phenobarb), benzodiazepines (e.g. Valium®, diazepam), cyanide, nicotine (from smoking), phencyclidine or morphine (a narcotic). The urine was tested for morphine, phencyclidine, cocaine, phenothiazines (antipsychotic drugs), methadone (a drug used in the treatment of narcotic withdrawal) and amphetamines, while the liver was tested for benzodiazepines and antidepressants. No positive findings were obtained.*

Death by "design"?

Just consider the time involved trying to determine the cause of John's death. They ruled out all the known possibilities. The list included all the common drugs of abuse usually encountered by their laboratory. Something else was obviously the cause of his death. Sixteen months later they retrieved the frozen post-mortem samples and determined death was due to a derivative of fentanyl (alpha-methylfentanyl), a derivative so potent that death required only a minute amount of the substance.

Designer Drugs Related to Meperidine (Demerol®)

Meperidine or Demerol® is another narcotic drug which, when used appropriately, is an effective substance for relief of severe pain. Chemists in clandestine or underground laboratories have produced analogues of this drug which are considerably more potent. In 1982, one analogue was detected, identified as MPPP (1-methyl-4-phenyl-4-propionoxy-piperidine). MPPP is about 5 to 10 times more potent as an analgesic (pain-relieving) than meperidine. Unfortunately, the process involved in making MPPP must be carefully controlled. This was not the case with samples prepared by the 'underground' chemists. On analysis, samples of MPPP have been found to contain MPTP (methylphenyltetrahydropyridine), a neurotoxic substance which damages nerve cells. In fact, this neurotoxin selectively destroys nerve cells in the brain. When this happens, the brain is not able to handle the brain chemical dopamine, resulting in Parkinsonism, a chronic nervous disorder marked by muscle rigidity. Parkinsonism usually occurs in people over 50 years of age. Therefore, doctors who were seeing young patients with the symptoms of this disease in its advanced stages were completely puzzled. These young patients appeared with bent-over posture, slow, almost rigid, movements and had difficulty speaking. It turned out these patients were users of designer drugs. Some reports suggest the damage produced by MPTP is **irreversible** and appears to worsen with time. Autopsy findings in one death revealed that MPTP had destroyed the nerve cells in the area of the brain that plays a major role in controlling movement.

Other derivatives of meperidine have also been associated with toxic by-products chemically related to the neurotoxin, MPTP. The problems caused by these derivatives and their by-products have literally created nightmares for many families and health professionals.

It is disturbing to know there are individuals out there trying to make a 'fast buck' at the expense of innocent individuals. There is no way this kind of practice should be tolerated. Developing analogues which have never been tested for activity or side effects before being sold on the street is very scary! Young people and adults must be forewarned of the tremendous dangers associated with such practices in order to prevent others from dying or becoming permanently handicapped. Users can never be sure what they are buying from their source of supply. Even marijuana has been laced on occasion with potent chemicals so that the user will get more of a 'bang' out of the 'pot'. The problems associated with these so-called new chemicals verify that **designer drugs are indeed an engineering nightmare!**

LET'S SEE WHAT WE'VE LEARNED ABOUT DESIGNER DRUGS

What are designer drugs?

What are some of the names used for designer drugs?

What are some of the serious effects of designer drug use?

How do designer drugs differ from medications discovered by pharmaceutical companies?

HEROIN & OTHER NARCOTICS

BEWARE OF STREET 'JUNK'!

HEROIN AND OTHER NARCOTICS

Beware of Street 'Junk'!

The naturally occurring opiates, such as morphine, are obtained from the latex-like substance secreted by the opium poppy, Papaver somniferum. Heroin, a derivative of morphine, is prepared by chemical reactions on poppy extracts and is thus referred to as a semi-synthetic compound (partially natural and partially chemically synthesized). Heroin has the greatest addiction potential of the narcotics and is probably the most widely abused of all opiates.

A narcotic is defined as a drug that, in small doses, dulls the senses, relieves pain, and induces profound sleep, but in excessive doses, causes stupor, coma, or convulsions.

Although heroin abuse was once prevalent in the adult population, in recent years younger people have become involved. A few case studies will verify that one of the street names for heroin ('junk') is quite appropriate.

> *Peter had been on the streets since he was 15 years old. Because his arms were like pin cushions he used to inject heroin under his tongue to avoid the tell-tale sign of the needle marks. He would not admit he had a drug problem.*

> *Charlie, a 20-year-old, arrived on the drug scene when he was just 13 years old, with the use of marijuana, Speed, and LSD. From these drugs he graduated to 'cocktails' of Speed and cocaine or a mixture of heroin and methylene-dioxyamphetamine (MDA). He then ran away from home and turned to prostitution to support his habit. According to last reports, Charlie was in his second year of rehabilitation.*

> *Ryan was 18 years old when he was admitted to the hospital for treatment of drug addiction. He had a long history of drug abuse beginning when he was just 14 years of age. He started on marijuana but subsequently found amphetamines gave him a lift and would allow him to 'talk for hours'. As the effect of amphetamines began to wear off, he felt 'down' and would try to compensate for this feeling by smoking marijuana. At 16 years of age Ryan started using heroin by injecting a small quantity, but soon found he could mix cocaine with the heroin for an even greater effect. Some time later, Ryan was sent to prison for three months after pleading guilty to marijuana possession. Although he resolved not to take drugs after his release from prison, he resumed drug taking only eight hours after being let out. He went back to using cocaine, heroin and Speed. Not only did he use these drugs himself, he helped and encouraged other boys to inject heroin. Ryan also bought and sold heroin, sometimes 'cutting' it with saccharin to make it go further.*

History

China was the first country where the social problems of opium became evident. By 1906, it was estimated that 20% of the adult Chinese population smoked opium and that 40 million were addicted.

Opium use spread to the West as a result of two major scientific advances. In 1805, the active components, codeine and morphine, were isolated from the opium poppy. This discovery provided a means for treatment in the withdrawal from opium poppy addiction. Little did they realize morphine and codeine were addictive themselves! The introduction of the hypodermic needle in 1843 was another contributing factor to the spread of opium use. The first of many narcotic addiction periods began in the United States following the Civil War. During the war, morphine was routinely administered to the wounded to relieve pain. When these soldiers returned to civilian life after the war, many found themselves needing the drug to survive and realized they were addicted. This addiction was therefore sometimes referred to as 'Soldiers' disease'.

During the nineteenth century, opium derivatives came under strict legal control with the passage of the Harrison Narcotic Act in the United States and the Narcotic Control Act in Canada. Although the number of people using opium-derived narcotics in the United States was quite low in the early 1900s, by 1964 a new epidemic started and has continued to this day.

Illegal Use of Heroin

In the 1980s, there was a sudden increase in heroin use, both in Canada and the United States. In 1983, a study conducted by the Addiction Research Foundation in Toronto, Canada found heroin use increased by 1000% from the previous year. During that year, Canada spent approximately $2.8 billion on heroin-related problems. Seizures by the federal police force (RCMP) were up by 233%. On the streets of Toronto alone, there was more heroin sold than the entire country had seen in the six previous years. One in every 70 students from seventh- to thirteenth-grade was also using heroin. The heaviest use was found in the 14- to 17-year-old age groups. Equally distressing was that 12- and 13-year-old students also reported using the drug.

Not only did heroin use increase but so did the potency of the product. In the 1970s, heroin was available in concentrations averaging around 3.5%. Products now contain 15%, 20% or higher. China White and 'Persian Porcelain' are so-called 'street names' for products containing high concentrations of heroin. What is confusing is that China White and Persian Porcelain may actually be some other chemical (for example, designer drugs). Later in the 1980s, more potent products became available which were substituted for heroin, resulting in a faster progression towards physical deterioration (remember, growing tissues are more prone to the toxic effects of chemicals than are mature tissues). Even today, heroin abuse is killing more people than ever before. Heroin use is prevalent on the Canadian West Coast, particularly in Vancouver. Officials in that part of the country could certainly verify the serious effects caused by its use.

Heroin use usually begins after other drugs have been tried. Very rarely does one become a heroin addict as his/her first addiction. Users generally start by smoking, drinking, using marijuana and psychedelics such as LSD. One exception would be those persons who have become addicted from the related drugs used for medical reasons (for example, codeine or morphine).

Narcotic use robs you of good health.

Stages of Narcotic Addiction

Initial Phase, sometimes referred to as the 'experimental phase', involves the first use of narcotics. As the individual continues to use the drug, they enter the second phase.

Maintenance Phase involves more frequent use of the drug in order to maintain the drug 'high'.

Continuing Phase is the phase in which the user cannot break the habit. Not only is there a continual desire to experience the euphoria or orgasmic feeling that the drug provides, but the user undergoes very unpleasant withdrawal symptoms if they try to stop their drug use. In other words, the user is 'hooked'.

The Effects of Heroin and Other Narcotics on The Body

Heroin is almost always administered by intravenous injection so that its effects begin almost immediately with an orgasmic rush, followed by euphoria and tranquillity. If an excess amount of the drug has been injected, a triad of events (three noticeable clinical symptoms) becomes evident. These symptoms are helpful in the diagnosis of narcotic drug use.

The triad includes: i) central nervous system depression,
ii) miosis – constriction of the pupils, and
iii) respiratory depression.

Along with this triad, needle tracks on the arms are also usually evident, although Peter tried to avoid this by injecting into the tongue area (see story at the start of this chapter). Often the arms are so badly scarred from injecting, addicts have to use other places to get the drug into the body such as the feet, the penis, or other parts of the body not already scarred from repeated injections.

Heroin and other narcotics paradoxically depress and stimulate the central nervous system, depending on the dosage. The individual experiences analgesia (pain relief) and/or euphoric effects, as well as sedative and hypnotic (sleep-inducing) effects. The respiratory centre is also depressed. With high dosages the general excitation of the central nervous system may lead to convulsions. Other effects include cold and clammy skin, hypothermia (decreased body temperature), decreased urine output, nausea and vomiting, pupil constriction (one of the tell-tale signs of narcotic use), slowing of the heart (which can lead to low blood pressure) and, in the severely poisoned individual, circulatory collapse, cardiac arrest and death.

Narcotic users are quite often constipated. This can also happen with prescription and over-the-counter pain relievers, which contain codeine. The reason for the constipation is a decrease in motility of the gastrointestinal system caused by the narcotic drugs.

Other serious medical consequences resulting from narcotic abuse include the development of numerous infections, including tetanus, inflammation of the area surrounding the heart, inflammation of the liver (hepatitis), and even HIV infection. Often these complications are a result of using dirty needle or perhaps due to a combination of both dirty needles and a contaminated drug. It is very rare for pure drugs to be sold on the street. There wouldn't be enough profit for the seller! Combined with all these problems, the overall health of the narcotic user is poor. This is due to an inadequate diet and the lack of proper nutrition; food is secondary to the abuser – drugs are all that matter.

Frequently, abusers overdose because of the high variability in heroin concentrations purchased on the street. Many addicts have overestimated the amount of the drug their body can handle, perhaps because they did not realize the potency of the product they purchased had increased. The user thus quickly passes into respiratory arrest and ultimately, to death.

Tolerance and Withdrawal

The rapid development of tolerance and the severity of the withdrawal effects from heroin and the other narcotics reinforce the continued need for narcotics. Tolerance leads to the never-ending need to increase the dose to achieve the euphoric effects and, most importantly, to avoid withdrawal symptoms. Withdrawal symptoms begin within a few hours after taking the last dose. The symptoms include watery eyes and runny nose, uncontrollable yawning, chills, goose bumps, and piloerection (the hair on the arms and legs appears to stand on end). These symptoms are probably responsible for the term 'cold turkey' which is used to describe someone 'coming off' narcotics. Muscle pain and spasms, involuntary leg movements ('kicking the habit') cramps, tremors, inability to sleep, nausea, vomiting, diarrhea, increased pupil size, increases in blood pressure, heart rate, respiration rate, and body temperature are a number of the unpleasant withdrawal symptoms. The male addict may experience

149

penile erections (often painful) and premature ejaculation of seminal fluid. The female addict may experience the occasional orgasm. Generally, the addict finds many of the withdrawal symptoms unbearable and will do anything to get more drug as a means of avoiding them. In a hospital setting, a physician will often prescribe medications to decrease the severity of the withdrawal effects.

Because heroin addicts find it hard to stop taking the drug, the relapse rate has been reported to be as high as 80% to 90%. In other words, this type of addiction is very hard to treat and is a real challenge for rehabilitation staff.

Crime Associated with Narcotic Use

The high costs associated with maintaining a heroin habit is often linked with crime. One must realize, however, that crime is not only associated with the abuse of narcotics. The same could apply to marijuana if the user was experiencing a cash flow problem. It has been reported that 30% to 40% of all heroin is purchased with money obtained as a result of burglaries, robberies, shoplifting and other non-violent crimes.

With respect to violence, heroin is rarely involved. Studies conducted in the 1970s suggest the opiate user is less likely to commit homicide, rape, or assault than are alcohol, amphetamine and barbiturate addicts. One study reported heroin addicts prefer to commit non-violent crimes (e.g. shoplifting) over violent crimes (e.g. armed robbery). The reason for these tendencies may be related to the tranquilizing effects of the drug.

Other Narcotics

Most of the preceding discussion focussed on heroin use. The opium poppy, Papaver somniferum, contains at least 25 different substances known as alkaloids. The main narcotic alkaloids are morphine and codeine. Chemical manipulation of morphine produces heroin, the more potent narcotic. Other chemical manipulations result in the formation of hydromorphone, oxymorphone, hydrocodone and oxycodone. All of these products, if taken in sufficient quantity, produce the signs and symptoms similar to those seen with heroin. Codeine is less addictive and is found in small quantities as one component in a

Drug habits are often linked with crime.

number of prescription and over-the-counter preparations. Deaths due to codeine are infrequent.

The above narcotics are referred to as 'natural' or 'semisynthetic'. They are produced by starting with a natural narcotic obtained from its plant source and then altering the structure, if necessary, by chemical manipulation. There are also other narcotics produced entirely by chemical means. The best known example of these is meperidine or Demerol®. The addiction potential of this narcotic is also relatively high.

Unfortunately, the street value for some of the prescription narcotics is high. To support their abuse, addicts will visit physicians for the sole purpose of obtaining a narcotic, which they can sell to someone else. Addicts also have their contacts. In one part of Canada, four individuals were charged after consulting 300 physicians and obtaining 40,000 narcotic tablets from 1100 pharmacies. The street value of the tablets was estimated to be between $2 and $3 million. Addicts try various means to get the drug. Forged prescriptions are not uncommon. Addicts will also feign (act out) a serious medical problem which would require a prescription for a narcotic. They are such good actors that the symptoms are portrayed with amazing accuracy, which may fool many doctors. Weekends are times commonly used by addicts to try and catch the doctors off-guard, often in crowded emergency departments. It is often difficult for physicians to keep up with the trends.

Heroin purchased on the street is never pure. It is 'cut' with any number of chemicals. This lack of purity may scare addicts into deciding to turn to prescription narcotics. At least the purity of the product is known.

Narcotic abuse is still rampant. When one examines all the serious problems that can develop from the abuse of these drugs, it should make one thankful they never got started on this or any other drug habit. Remember, unlike pharmaceutical manufacturers, drug pushers are not required to submit their products for quality assurance tests, so we can safely assume that drugs purchased on the street are never pure. Not knowing the purity makes overdosing a real possibility. One overdose is all it takes! If an overdose does not happen, the individual may become ill from the impurities found in the street samples. And what about the needles used to inject the drug? Sharing syringes and needles is known to be the cause of many diseases, including those affecting the liver, blood, heart, brain and is also a contributing factor for AIDS. **Beware of this 'junk'!**

LET'S SEE WHAT YOU'VE LEARNED ABOUT NARCOTICS

What is a narcotic?

What is the triad of effects that may be seen when someone uses a narcotic?

What are some of the effects of narcotic use on the skin, on respiration, heart beat and the eyes?

Why is one of the effects of withdrawal after using narcotics called 'cold turkey'?

Are there any narcotic drugs that you get by prescription or in over-the-counter medications?

STEROIDS

WHY THE RAGE ABOUT 'ROIDS'?

STEROIDS

Why The Rage About 'Roids'?

Steroids and sports became big news in 1988 when urine collected from Olympic sprinter, Ben Johnson, tested positive for an illegal substance. To have his gold medal stripped was devastating not only for him but for Canada, the country he proudly represented. Why did he do it? What are the possible side effects of such a practice? How do we convince our youth not to take steroids when celebrities have been using them for years? These, as well as other questions, become foremost in many minds. Even though this section will deal with the possible devastating effects of anabolic steroids, it should not be forgotten that steroids can still be prescribed by physicians for legitimate medical reasons, with positive results. Medically, steroids are often prescribed for a short period of time with no side effects. For some other conditions, the patient may need steroids on a continuing basis. In this latter instance, side effects may occur but are closely monitored by the physician.

Steroids, if used inappropriately, could produce any one of the following devastating effects.

> *John, a 23-year-old bodybuilder, complained of severe groin pain and was taken to the hospital for treatment. The doctors found that his liver and kidneys had stopped working. He was rushed to the intensive care unit. Four days later, he died from heart failure. His autopsy revealed he was a steroid abuser.*

156

Bill, a world class power weightlifter with no past history of heart disease, was admitted to the hospital with severe chest pain. The pain had awakened him from his sleep. He had being using intramuscular and oral steroids daily during the 6 weeks prior to developing the chest pain. This athlete had developed very high cholesterol levels. Steroids, power lifting and dietary factors may have been contributing factors causing spasm of the artery leading to the heart.

Ken, an amateur bodybuilder, was convicted of second-degree murder. Three months before committing the crime, he had started taking anabolic steroids on the advice of friends at the gym. He had been assured that there were no adverse effects. Personality changes became evident. Ken became 'hyper' and irritable. He quarrelled noisily and started consuming increasing amounts of alcohol. One night while talking with his girlfriend, Ken 'snapped'. His girlfriend was severely beaten and died as the result of a massive blood clot. Testimony at Ken's trial revealed he had become a changed man after he began using steroids.

While Ted was preparing for his high school prom night, he drank a health formula that was promoted as an anabolic steroid-alternative, which he was using to increase muscle and reduce fat. His evening of romance was not to be. Twenty minutes after drinking the substance he lapsed into a coma. His parents found him on the floor and rushed him to the hospital. The doctors said if he had been found 30 minutes later, he probably would have died.

The stories of John, Bill, Ken and Ted are disturbing, but not unusual. Many athletes will 'push' these drugs because of the increased body strength they provide. This makes them popular to both men and women who want to increase muscle mass and muscle definition. According to the FDA Consumer (September 1991), abuse is related to the fact that young men feel they need to look 'masculine' – strong and muscular. Young people are not concerned about the long-term effects – they just want to make that team and be popular – they'll worry later about possible damage to the liver, heart and other organs. In fact, most feel they don't have to worry because they will certainly stop using steroids before it is too late.

What are Anabolic Steroids?

Anabolic steroids include the naturally occurring sex hormone, testosterone, and its chemical derivatives. In males, testosterone is responsible for the development and maintenance of secondary sexual characteristics including facial and pubic hair growth and deepening of the voice. In females, where testosterone is present in significantly smaller amounts, it is again responsible for the development of some secondary sexual characteristics such as hair growth in the pubic and armpit regions. These are referred to as the androgenic or masculinizing effects of testosterone.

Testosterone also possesses anabolic or tissue-building effects. It promotes tissue growth by stimulating protein production and slowing its breakdown in body tissues.

History and Prevalence of Use

Since the first anabolic steroids were prepared in the laboratory, these drugs have been used to treat a variety of medical conditions. Some of these include the treatment of osteoporosis (a disease characterized by a loss of bone tissue), anemias (conditions in which there is a decrease in red blood cells), hypogonadism (improper functioning of the testes) in young males and short stature.

Not long after its discovery and isolation in 1936, testosterone was first used for non-medicinal purposes. During World War II, it is believed that the Nazis injected their troops with testosterone in order to make them more aggressive during combat.

It has been suggested that as early as 1953, testosterone was administered to Russian athletes in an attempt to enhance their athletic performance. It did not take long for athletes to start abusing these drugs; some were taking 20 times the recommended doses. Abuse led to the development of liver problems in a few of the athletes. Because of this, the use of steroids in sports was banned.

Since the 1950s there has been a phenomenal increase in the use of anabolic steroids by athletes. In 1968, the International Olympic Committee banned steroid use and, in 1976, routine urine testing for banned substances was initiated. Prior to 1983, most samples collected were subjected to what was referred to as 'sink testing', that is, testing procedures were not very sophisticated and many samples were washed down the drain. Because no one seemed to get caught, testing did not deter athletes from using steroids and use continued to increase.

With more sophisticated testing techniques, 19 athletes in the 1983 Venezuela Pan American Games were disqualified due to detection of steroids in their urine. Testing procedures had improved dramatically and were sensitive to the detection of small concentrations present in blood and urine.

The actual number of athletes using anabolic steroids is not known. According to the Committee on Doping in Amateur Sport, only 5% of athletes in Canada used steroids in 1980. Other studies suggest that this is an underestimation and have provided the following usage levels – approximately 98% of all male bodybuilders and powerlifters, including Olympic weightlifters, are believed to use anabolic steroids. Fifty to ninety percent of athletes involved in sports such as track and field and football are suspected of using anabolic steroids to improve their performance. These figures are a far cry from the 1980 estimate of 5%.

Over the past few years, illicit use of steroids has become widespread. Elite athletes are no longer exclusive users of these drugs. Users now include both non-competitive athletes and non-athletes, with use beginning as early as junior high school. A recent study of the prevalence of anabolic steroid use in American high school students indicates about 7% of male students are anabolic steroid users.

How Anabolic Steroids are Used

Anabolic steroids are taken either orally, often in tablet form, or by injection. The testes in the healthy male produce approximately 8 milligrams of testosterone each day. Medicinal doses of anabolic steroids vary depending on the preparation and reason for use. For example, testosterone propionate, when used for hormone replacement therapy, is administered by intramuscular injection in dosages of 10 to 50 milligrams three times a week. Abusers, on the other hand, take megadoses, often 10 to 100 times the recommended therapeutic doses.

> *Paul, a 24-year-old non-competitive weightlifter, was admitted into a psychiatric unit after he asked for professional help to quit taking steroids. He complained of being depressed and said that he had considered suicide. Paul felt these feeling were related to his use of steroids. At the time of his admission, Paul was taking 200 milligrams of testosterone cypionate intramuscularly every 3 days, 100 milligrams of nandrolone decanoate intramuscularly every 3 days, 25 milligrams of oxandrolone orally daily, 40 milligrams of methandrostenolone orally daily, 30 to 45 milligrams of bolasterone subcutaneously every 2 to 3 days and 1000 to 2000 units of human chorionic gonadotrophin intramuscularly every 2 to 3 days.*

There are three main methods of administration used by athletes and other steroid abusers: 'stacking', 'cycling', and 'pyramiding'. 'Stacking' refers to the simultaneous use of a number of different steroids. Paul (above) was taking 5 different preparations. 'Cycling' involves alternating periods of steroid use with steroid-free periods. The anabolic steroid user will take the drugs for a period of 6 to 12 weeks and then take a 'drug holiday' for 1 to 12 months. 'Pyramiding' is when cycles of steroid use are started at low doses and then the dosages are gradually increased. These methods are employed in an attempt to minimize side effects and prevent development of tolerance to the effects of steroids on muscle tissue. Tolerance develops for many of the street drugs and users find they need higher doses to get the effects they initially experienced.

Effects of Anabolic Steroids on the Body

– Endocrine (Hormonal)

In females, deepening of the voice, increased growth of body hair, enlargement of the clitoris, decreased breast size, menstrual irregularities, and the development of male pattern baldness are all effects associated with anabolic steroid use. Collectively, these effects are referred to as 'masculinization'. Some of these effects are believed to be reversible once steroid use has ended. However, clitoral

160

enlargement, body hair growth, and male pattern baldness are considered irreversible.

In men, anabolic steroids may cause testicular atrophy (wasting away of testicular tissue), impotence, infertility and enlargement of the breasts. Testicular atrophy and infertility are probably reversible but breast growth is not readily reversed. In some cases, cosmetic surgery may be required to remove the breast tissue.

– The Liver

Liver damage is probably the most serious consequence of using anabolic steroids. A significant portion of patients taking therapeutic doses of oral anabolic steroids develops liver problems. One can imagine the results of taking megadoses of these drugs. Some specific liver disorders associated with prolonged anabolic steroid use include cholestatic jaundice (jaundice caused by a blocked bile duct), malignant (cancerous) tumours, and peliosis hepatitis (a condition in which blood-filled sacs form in the liver).

– Cardiovascular

Due to a negative effect on blood fat, anabolic steroids may increase the risk of developing atherosclerotic coronary artery disease if they are used for extended periods of time. Studies show that levels of the 'good' high-density lipoproteins (HDL) are lowered and levels of the 'bad' low-density lipoproteins (LDL) are raised in individuals using anabolic steroids. A high LDL/HDL ratio, like that produced by anabolic steroids, is associated with an increased risk of developing heart disease. Remember the story of Bill at the beginning of this chapter!

– Behavioural

Anabolic steroid use can cause changes in behaviour. These changes are most often seen as increased aggressiveness and irritability. Many steroid users recall at least one episode of unprovoked aggressive behaviour. These episodes are referred to as **'roid rages'**.

In extreme cases, symptoms of depression and psychoses (severe mental illness where a person loses contact with reality) may develop. These symptoms tend to increase during periods of steroid use and lessen once steroid use has ended.

> *Colin, a 23-year-old bodybuilder, purchased a new $17,000 sports car soon after he began a cycle of a steroid use. The payments on the car were steep. When friends who knew that he couldn't afford the payments questioned him about his purchase, Colin told them he had it all figured out and money was no problem. When he stopped the drug, Colin realized that he could not afford the payments and sold the car. About a year later, after starting another cycle of steroids, Colin bought another sports car on impulse. This car cost him $20,000.*

> *Darren, 19, was driving home from work one day when he noticed that the driver in the car in front of him had left his left signal light on. Darren found this to be extremely irritating – so much so that at the next red light he jumped out of his car and smashed the windshield of the car with the flashing signal.*

– Muscular & Skeletal

In children and adolescents, excessive steroid use causes premature fusion of the long bones which means these bones stop growing and full height development will not be reached.

Tendon damage is seen in many athletes who use steroids. This may be caused by a large increase in muscle power without a similar increase in tendon strength. The tendon cannot support the weight that the improved muscle can and so it is prone to snap! Others have suggested steroids inhibit the production of collagen, an important component of tendons and ligaments. Without collagen the tendon loses its strength and is easily ruptured. A third reason suggested by sports doctors is that the increased aggression, commonly seen in users of anabolic steroids, causes them to attempt to lift too much weight and to be less careful when doing so.

– Miscellaneous Effects

Other effects of steroids on the body include acne breakouts, water retention, headaches, increased appetite, increased risk of developing diabetes, and an increased risk of stroke. Steroid users also

162

have an increased risk of getting AIDS and hepatitis B since needles are often shared.

Of real concern is the fact that the body normally produces its own steroids in a balanced fashion. If steroids are taken from an external source, the body recognizes this as being too much and will shutdown its own steroid production process. If the person requires emergency surgery, becomes ill or suffers any other trauma, the steroids needed by the body are not produced (because the mechanism has shutdown). This could result in severe lowering of the blood pressure, shock, collapse and even death.

It is hard to imagine, with all the potential serious health effects associated with steroid use, why there has been such a **rage about 'roids'**.

LET'S SEE WHAT YOU'VE LEARNED ABOUT STEROIDS

Why were soldiers given steroids?

Why do young people/athletes use steroids?

What are the effects of steroids on the heart?

How many other health effects of steroid abuse can you list?

INTERNET RESOURCES*

substanceabuse.region.halton.on.ca
. . . . Halton Community Action for a Drug Free Youth
www.acde.org
. . . . American Council for Drug Education
www.americanheart.org
. . . . American Heart Association
www.arf.org
. . . . Addiction Research Foundation
www.ash.org
. . . . Action on Smoking and Health
www.casacolumbia.org
. . . . The National Center on Addiction and Substance
Abuse at Columbia University
www.ccs.ca
. . . . Canadian Cardiovascular Society
www.ccsa.ca
. . . . Canadian Centre on Substance Abuse
www.cdc.gov
. . . . Centers for Disease Control and Prevention
www.clubdrugs.org
. . . . National Institute on Drug Abuse
www.cts.com/crash/habtsmrt/family.htm
. . . . HabitSmart Family Page
www.daddac.com/main_frame.htm
. . . . DAD (Dogs Against Drugs)
www.Dare-America.com
. . . . Drug Abuse Resistance Education
www.drugabuse.ca
. . . . Council on Drug Abuse (CODA)
www.deal.org
. . . . Royal Canadian Mounted Police
www.drugfreeamerica.org
. . . . Drug-Free Resource Net
www.drugs.indiana.edu/resources/other_resources.html
. . . . Indiana Prevention Resource Center at Indiana University
www.edx.org/drugfreekids.shtml
. . . . DrugFree Kids (Drug Free USA)

www.fcd.org

. . . . FCD (Freedom from Chemical Dependency)
Educational Services Inc.

www.goaskalice.columbia.edu

. . . . Go Ask Alice! (Columbia University)

www.hc-sc.gc.ca/english

. . . . Health Canada Online

www.hc-sc.gc.ca/hppb/tobaccoreduction

. . . . Health Canada Online

www.health.org/kidsarea/kidsarea.htm

. . . . National Clearinghouse for Alcohol and Drug Information

www.health.org/pubs/catalog

. . . . National Clearinghouse for Alcohol and Drug Information

www.helix.com/helix/coned/shared/nicotine/index.htm

. . . . Helix Continuing Education (Glaxo Wellcome)

www.holycross.edu/departments/library/substanceabuse/page3.htm

. . . . Holy Cross Library Substance Abuse Page

www.kidsource.com

. . . . US Department of Education

www.netwellness.org

. . . . University of Cincinnati

www.nida.nih.gov

. . . . . . National Institute on Drug Abuse-National Institutes of Health

www.nida.nih.gov/Infofax/InfofaxIndex.html

. . . . National Institute on Drug Abuse

www.nida.nih.gov/MOM/MOMIndex.html

. . . . . . National Institute on Drug Abuse-National Institutes of Health

www.teacherpathfinder.org

. . . . Teacher Pathfinder

www.tobaccofacts.org

. . . . British Columbia Ministry of Health

www.tobaccofreekids.org

. . . . Campaign for Tobacco-Free Kids

www.tvo.org

. . . . TV Ontario

*The author would like to thank Ms. Arlene Salonga for permission to reproduce the list which appeared in her Hospital Residency Report – "Pharmacist Involvement in Drug Education for Elementary School-Aged Children" (St. Joseph's Health Centre, Toronto, August 1999).

SIGNS AND SYMPTOMS OF DRUG USE

It is important to note that the following is a list of possible signs and symptoms of drug use and that normal adolescent moods can resemble signs of drug use. It is also important that you be aware of any important changes in your child's life so you can assist him/her through a crisis. Be aware, alert and communicate with your child.

Physical Symptoms

- acting intoxicated
- drooping eyelids; red eyes; dilated or constricted pupils
- abnormally pale complexion
- change in sleep patterns such as insomnia, napping or sleeping at inappropriate times
- frequent illness due to lowered resistance to infection
- runny nose; hacking cough; persistent chest pains
- sudden changes in appetite, especially for sweets (munchies)
- unexplained weight loss or loss of appetite
- neglect of personal appearance, grooming

Behavioural and Personality Changes

- unexplained swings in mood, depression, anxiety and continued resentful behaviour
- inappropriate over-reaction to mild criticism or simple requests
- preoccupation with self, less concern for feelings of others
- secretiveness and withdrawal from family
- loss of interest in previously important things, e.g. hobbies, sports
- lack of motivation, boredom, 'I don't care' attitude
- lethargy, lack of energy, noticeable drop in attention span, short-term memory loss
- change in values, ideals, beliefs
- change in friends, unwillingness to introduce friends
- secretive phone calls, callers refuse to identify themselves or hang up when you answer
- periods of unexplained absence from home
- stealing money or articles which can be readily sold for cash
- wearing sunglasses at inappropriate times

Physical Evidence

- foil packaging
- odour of burnt rope (marijuana) on clothing or in room
- incense or room deodorizers
- eyedrops
- rolled or twisted cigarettes (possibly marijuana joints)
- roach clips (feather clips)
- powders, seeds, leaves, plant material, mushrooms
- unexplained capsules or tablets
- cigarette rolling papers
- pipes, pipe fittings
- water pipes, bong (usually glass or plastic and my have brown stains on the smoking end)
- weighing scales, testing kits
- small spoons, straws, razor blades, mirrors
- stash cans (pop cans or other cans that unscrew from the bottom)
- plastic baggies or small glass vials
- drug-related books, magazines (e.g. High Times), comics, Internet material
- knives with burnt ends
- propane torch

Many of the above items can be found, usually hidden, in the person's room or car. Some of the more ingenious places of concealment include the underside of dresser drawers, between mattresses, behind light switches, inside stereos, between book pages, or in clothing. More obvious locations include car trunks, pocketbooks, and closet shelves.

Observed School Changes

- decline in academic performance, drop in grades
- reduced short-term memory, concentration, attention span
- loss of motivation, participation in school activities
- frequent tardiness and absenteeism
- less interest in participating in class
- sleeping in class
- untidy appearance, dress, decreased personal hygiene
- apathy
- increased discipline, behavioural problems
- change in peer group

REFERENCES

ALCOHOL:

Depuis C et al. Les cardiopathies des enfants nés de mère alcoolique. Arch Mal Coeur 1978; 71:656-72.

Eckhardt MJ et al. Health hazards associated with alcohol consumption. JAMA 1981; 246:648-66.

Edmondson HA. Pathology of alcoholism. Am J Clin Pathol 1980; 74:725-42.

Gordon GG et al. Metabolic effects of alcohol on the endocrine system. In: Leiber S, ed. Metabolic Aspects of Alcoholism. Baltimore: University Park Press 1977:249-302.

Jones KL et al. Recognition of the fetal alcohol syndrome in early infancy. Lancet 1973; 2:999-1001.

Lee NM et al. The alcohols. In: Katzung BG, ed. Basic and Clinical Pharmacology. California: Lange Medical Publications 1982.

Lemoine P et al. Les enfants de parents alcooliques; anomalies observees à propos de 127 cas. Ouest Med 1968; 21:479-82.

Little RE et al. Decreased birthweight in infants of alcoholic women who abstained during pregnancy. J Pediatr 1980; 96:974-77.

Loser H et al. Type and frequency of cardiac defects in embryo-fetal alcohol syndrome. Report of 16 cases. Br Heart J 1977; 39:1374-79.

Lyons HA et al. Diseases of the respiratory tract in alcoholics. In: Kissin B, Begleiter H, eds. The Biology of Alcoholism: Clinical Pathology. New York: Plenum Press Inc. 1974; 3:402-4

Malcolm JB et al. Alcohol intoxication: An underdiagnosed problem? Arch of Dis in Childhood 1985; 60:762-3.

MacDonald DI. Drugs, drinking and adolescents: Chicago: Yearbook, Medical Publishers, 1984; 68-72.

McDermott PH et al. Myocardosis and cardiac failure in man. JAMA 1966; 198:253-6.

Morin Y et al. Quebec beer-drinker's cardiomyopathy: etiological considerations. Can Med Assoc J 1967; 97: 926-8.

Morris AI. Sexuality, alcohol and liver disease. In: Krasner N, Madden JS and Walker RJ, eds. Alcohol-Related Problems. New York: John Wiley Sons Ltd. 1984:251-6.

Russel M. Intrauterine growth in infants born to women with alcohol-related psychiatric disorders. Alcoholism 1977; l:224-31.

Ryback RS. Chronic alcohol consumption and menstruation. JAMA 1977; 238:2143.

Sandyk R et al. Transient Gilles de la Tourette Syndrome following alcohol withdrawal. Br J Addiction 1985; 80:213-14.

Saskatchewan Alcohol and Drug Abuse Commission. Alcohol, Drugs and Youth – Report of the Minister's Advisory Committee. 1986.

Seixas FA et al. Definition of alcoholism. Ann Int Med 1976; 85:764.

Shanks J. Alcohol and Youth. World Health Forum 1990;11:235-241.

Shaywitz SE et al. Behaviour and learning difficulties in children of normal intelligence born to alcoholic mothers. J Pediatr 1980; 96:978-82.

Sokol RT et al. Alcohol abuse during pregnancy: an epidemiologic study. Alcoholism 1980; 4:134-45.

Sulivan WC. A note on the influence of maternal inebriety on the offspring. J Ment Sci 1981; 45:489-503.

U.S. Department of Health and Human Services. Sixth Special Report to the U. S. Congress on Alcohol and Health. January 1987: pp. xvii-xviii.

Van Thiel DH et al. Ethanol: a gonadal toxin in the female. Drug Alcohol Depend 1977; 2:373-80.

AMPHETAMINES AND HALLUCINOGENS:

Addiction Research Foundation, Toronto Dial-a-Fact, Transcript 222.

Burns RS et al. Causes of phencyclidine related deaths. Clin Toxicol 1978; 12:463-81.

Casey FC. Drugs of Abuse-The Facts. PCP – the 'garbage' drug of the streets. Fact Sheet.

Check FE et al. Deceptions in the illicit drug market. Science 1970; 167:1276.

Cohen S et al. Prolonged adverse reactions to lysergic acid diethylamide. Archives Gen Psych 1963; 8:475-80.

Cohen S. The hallucinogens and the inhalants. Psychiatr Clinics N Am 1984; 7:681-88.

Dewhurst, K. Psilocybin intoxication. Br J Psychiatr 1980; 137:303-4.

Duquesne University-School of Pharmacy. Pittsburgh: The Toxicology Newsletter 1987; 13.

Ellenhorn MJ and Barceloux DG, eds. Medical Toxicology – Diagnosis and Treatment of Human Poisoning. Part III – Drugs of Abuse. New York: Elsevier, 1988:626-777.

Fauman B et al. Psychiatric sequelae of phencyclidine abuse. Clin Toxicol 1976; 9:529-38.

Fink PJ et al. Morning glory seed. Psychosis Arch Gen Psychiatr 1966; 15:209-11

Fuller DG. Severe solar maculopathy associated with the use of lysergic acid diethylamide. Am J Ophthamol 1976; 81:413-16.

Herskowitz J et al. More about poisoning by phencyclidine ('PCP', 'Angel Dust'). N Eng J Med 1977; 297:1405.

Hofmann FG. Hallucinogens: LSD and agents having similar effects. In: A Handbook on Drug and Alcohol Abuse. New York: Oxford University Press, 1975; 149.

Hollister L. Drugs of Abuse. In: Katzung BG, ed. Basic and Clinical Pharmacology. California: Lange Medical Publications, 1984:353-65.

Hollister LE. Effects of hallucinogens in humans. In: Jacobs BL, ed. Central Nervous System Pharmacology Series. Hallucinogens: Neurochemical Behavioural and Clinical Perspectives. New York: Raven Press, 1984:19-33.

Hong, R et al. Cardiomyopathy associated with the smoking of crystal methamphetamine. JAMA 1991; 265(9):1152-54.

Honolulu Advertiser, Feb 5, 1989 and August 4, 1990.

Jackson, J. G. Hazards of Smokable Methamphetamine. N Eng J Med 1989; 32:907.

Keeler MH et al. Suicide during an LSD reaction. Amer J Psychiatr 1967; 123:884-85.

Litovitz T. Hallucinogens. In: Haddad LM, Winchester JF, eds. Clinical Management of Poisoning and Drug Overdose. Toronto: WB Saunders Co., 1985:455-66.

Mack, RB. The Iceman Cometh and Killeth: Smokable Methamphetamine. NCMJ 1990; 51(6):276-78.

National Drug Intelligence Estimate 1988-89. Drug Enforcement Directorate, RCMP Headquarters, Ottawa, Canada.

Nesson DR et al. An analysis of psychedelic flashbacks. Am J Drug Alcohol Abuse 3:425-35.

Peden NR et al. Hallucinogenic fungi. Lancet 1982; i

Poklis A et al. Fatal intoxication from 3,4-methylenedioxyamphetamine. J Forens Sci 1979; 24:70.

Richards KC et al. Near fatal reaction to ingestion of the hallucinogenic drug MDA. JAMA 1971; 218:1826-7.

Shulgin AT et al. Illicit synthesis of phencyclidine (PCP) and several of its analogues. Clin Toxicol 1976; 9:553-60.

Simpson DI et al. Methylenedioxyamphetamine: Clinical description of overdose, death, and review of pharmacology. Arch Int Med 1981; 141:1507.

Sioris LJ et al. Phencyclidine intoxication: A literature review. Am J Hosp Pharm 1978; 35:1362-7.

Smith DE et al. The use and abuse of LSD in Haight-Ashbury. Clin Pediatr 1968; 7:317.

Solursh LP et al. Hallucinogenic drug abuse: Manifestations and Management. Can Med Assoc J 1968; 98:407.

Thiessen PN et al. The properties of 3,4-methylenedioxyamphetamine (MDA) I. A review of the literature. Clin Toxicol 1973; 6:45-52.

Ungerleider TJ et al. The 'bad trip'. The etiology of the adverse LSD reaction. Am J Psychiat 1968; 124:1483-90.

Wessen, DR and Washburn P. Current Patterns of Drug Abuse that Involve Smoking. NIDA Research Monograph 99:5-11.

COCAINE:

Aldrich MR et al. Historical aspects of cocaine use and abuse. In: Mule AJ, ed. Cocaine: Chemical, Biological, Clinical, Social and Treatment aspects. Ohio: CRC Press, 1976.

Anderson B. Drug Update: What is 'Crack'? Newsletter of the National Federation of Parents (NFP), Washington, DC.

Ashley R, ed. Cocaine: Its history, uses and effects. New York: St. Martin's Press, 1975.

Byck R, ed. Cocaine Papers: Sigmund Freud. New York: Stone Hill Publishing Co., 1983.

Cohen S. Cocaine. JAMA 1975; 231:74-5.

DeLeon G. An intervention model. In: deSilva R, Dupont RL, Russel GK, eds. Treating the Marihuana Dependent Person. Rockville: American Council for Drug Education, 1981:44-8.

Gold, MS. 800-Cocaine. New York: Bantam Books Inc., 1985.

Gutierrez N et al. Cocainismo Experimental I. Toxicologica general acostumoramieto y sensibilazacion (Experimental Cocainism I. General toxicology, habituation and sensitization. Rev de Med Exp 1944; 3:279-304.

Haddad, LM. Cocaine. In: Clinical Management of Poisoning and Drug Overdose. Haddad LM, Winchester JF, eds. Toronto: WB Saunders Co., 1983:443-7.

Hollister L. Drugs of Abuse. In: Katzung BD, ed. Basic and Clinical Pharmacology. California, Lange Medical Publications, 1984.

Kulburg A. Substance abuse: Clinical identification and management. Pediatr Toxicol 1986; 33:325-61.

MacDonald I. Drugs, drinking and adolescents. Chicago: Yearbook Medical Publishers, 1984.

MacLeans Magazine. The high and crippling cost of cocaine. June 17, 1985.

Maiiani A, ed. Cola and Its Therapeutic Application. New York: Taros, 1980.

Meyers JA et al. Generalized seizures and cocaine abuse. Neurology 1984; 34:675-76.

Moore DC. Complication of regional anesthesia. In: Bonica JS, ed. Regional Anesthesia. Philadelphia: WB Saunders, 1969:217-53.

Newsweek magazine. June 30, 1986.

Petersen RC et al. Cocaine 1977. NIDA Research Monograph 13. National Institute on Drug Abuse. Washington, DC: US Government Printing office, 1977.

Shesser R et al. Pneumomediastinum and Pneumothorax after inhaling alkaloidal cocaine. Ann Emerg Med 1981; 10:213-15.

Siegel RK Cocaine Use and driving behaviour. Alcohol, Drugs and Driving 1985; 3:1-7.

Teri FR et al. The syndrome of coca paste. J Psychedel Drugs 1978; 10:361-70.

Thompson T et al. Stimulant self-administration by animals: Some comparisons with opiate administration. Federal Proc 1970; 29:6-12.

VanDyke C et al. Cocaine 1884-1974. In: Ellinwood EH, Kilbey MD, eds. Cocaine and other stimulants. New York: Plenum Press, 1977.

Vilensky WDO. Illicit and licit drugs causing perforation of the nasal septum. J Forens Sci 1982; 27:956-62.

Weiss RD et al. Pulmonary dysfunction in cocaine smokers. Am J Psychiatr 1981; 138:1110-12.

DESIGNER DRUGS:

Buchanan JF, Brown CR. 'Designer Drugs' A Problem in Clinical Toxicology. Med Toxicol 1988; 3:1-17.

Ellenhorn MJ, Barceloux DG, eds. Medical Toxicology- Diagnosis and Treatment of Human Poisoning, New York: Elsevier, 1988:689-762.

National Federation of Parents (NFP), Washington, DC. Newsletters and Bulletins.

DRUG USE IN THE NEW MILLENNIUM:

Centre for Addiction and Mental Health. Ontario Student Drug Use Survey – Executive Summary 1999. www.camh.net/understanding/ont_study_drug_use.html

Gilkeson RC. The Toxicity of Intoxicants is not determined by debate. Drug Watch International:the organization, position statements, and other papers. 2000 edition

PRIDE Canada Inc., Press Release. Teen Drug Use Remains At "All Time High". January 1998.

Single E et al. The Costs of Substance Abuse in Canada. Highlights of a major study of the health, social and economic costs associated with the use of alcohol, tobacco and illicit drugs. Canadian Centre on Substance Abuse. http://www.ccsa.ca

Stocker, S. Overall Teen Drug Use Stays Level, Use of MDMA and Steroids Increases. NIDA Notes (National Institute on Drug Abuse) 2000;15(1):5

ECSTASY (MDMA):

Bolla KI et al. Memory impairment in abstinent MDMA ("Ecstasy") users. Neurology 1998; 51:1532-7.

Brauer, RB et al. Liver transplantation for the treatment of fulminant hepatic failure induced by the ingestion of ecstasy. Transpl. Int. 1997;10:229-233.

Mas, M et al. Cardiovascular and neuroendocrine effects and pharmacokinetics of 3,4-methylenedioxymethamphetamine in humans. J. Pharmacol. Exp. Ther. 1999; 290: 136-45.

McCann UD. Cognitive performance in (+/-) 3,4-methylenedioxymethamphetamine (MDMA, "ecstasy") users: a controlled study. Psychopharmacology 1999; 143:417-25.

Merrill, J. Ecstasy and neurodegeneration. BMJ 1996;313:423

Milosevic, A et al. The occurrence of toothwear in users of Ecstasy. Community Dent. Oral Epidemiol. 1999; 27:283-7.

Milroy CM. Ten years of 'ecstasy'. J. Royal Soc. Med 1999; 92:68-71.

Morgan MJ. Memory deficits associated with recreational use of "ecstasy" (MDMA). Psychopharmacology 1999; 141:30-6.

National Institute on Drug Abuse, INFOFAX Ecstasy 13547 – http://www.drugabuse.gov/

Rochester JA and Kirchner JT. Ecstasy (3,4-methylenedioxymethamphetamine): history, neurochemistry, and toxicology. J. Am. Board Fam. Pract.1999; 12:137-42.

Schlaeppi, M et al. Cerebral hemorrhage and "ecstasy". Schweiz Rundsch Med. Prax. 1999;88:568-72

Schwartz, RH, and Miller NS. MDMA (Ecstasy) and the Rave: a Review. Pediatrics 1997;100:705-708.

Sherlock K et al. Analysis of illicit ecstasy tablets: implications for clinical management in the accident and emergency department. J. Accid. Emerg.Med 1999; 16:194-7.

Toronto Star, February 1, 2000 – Teens busted after record Ecstasy haul at Pearson.

Toronto Star, February 26, 2000 – Drug lords find Toronto pure ecstasy.

Toronto Star, March 5, 2000 – Man killed in rave club shooting.

Williams H et al. "Saturday night fever":ecstasy related problems in a London accident and emergency department. J Accid. Emerg Med. 1998;15:322-6.

HEROIN AND OTHER NARCOTICS

Alcohol and Drug Use Among Ontario Students (News Release). Toronto: Alcoholism and Drug Addiction Foundation. Jan 5,1985 in: Alcohol, Drugs and Youth – report of the Minister's Advisory Committee (Government Publication).

Ball JC et al. Absence of major medical complications among chronic opiate addicts. Br J Addict 1970; 65:109-12.

Cohen S,ed. The Drug Dilemma. New York: McGraw-Hill Book Co., 1969:69-83.

Gossop MR. Addiction to narcotics: A brief review of 'Junkie' literature. Br J Addict 1976; 71:192-5.

Heroin Maintenance: The Issues. Washington DC: The Drug Abuse Council Inc., June 1973. (Second printing; Feb 1975).

Hollister L: Drugs of abuse. In: Katzung BG, ed. Basic and Clinical Pharmacology. California: Lange Medical Publications, 1984:453-64.

Kraft T. Drug addiction and personality disorder. Br J Addiction 1970; 64:403-8.

MacDonald DI. Drugs, drinking and adolescents. Chicago: Year Book Medical Publishers, 1984.

Merry J. A social history of heroin addiction. Br J Addiction 70:307-10.

Moore M, ed. Policy Concerning Drug Abuse in New York State – Vol III: Economics of heroin distribution. New York: Croton-on-Hudson, Hudson Institute, 1970:65.

The Globe and Mail. December 19, 1984.

Toronto Star. January 6, 1984.

Toronto Star. Some kids learn dangers of heroin or cocaine addiction the hard way. November 12, 1984.

MARIJUANA:

Abel EL, ed. Marijuana: The first twelve thousand years. New York: Plenum Press, 1980:237-59.

Barry H III et al. Delta 1-Tetrahydrocannabinol activation of pituitary-adrenal function. Pharmacologist 1970; 12:327.

Dalterio S. Marijuana and the unborn. Presentation at the First National Conference on Drugs and Youth, PRIDE Canada Inc.

Klonhoff H. Acute psychological effects in man, including acute cognitive, psychomotor and perceptual effects on driving. In: Adverse Health and Behavioural Consequences of Cannabis. Working Papers for the ARF/WHO Scientific Meeting. Fehr KO, Kala H, eds. Toronto: Addiction Research Foundation 1983.

Kolansky H et al. Effects of marijuana on adolescents and young adults. JAMA 1971; 216:

Kolody RC et al. Depression of plasma testosterone with acute marijuana administration. In: Pharmacology of Marijuana. McBrauded MC, Szara S, ed. New York: Raven Press, 1976:277.

MacDonald DI, comp. Drugs, Drinking and Adolescents. Chicago: Year Book Medical Publishers, 1984.

Marijuana – Its Health Hazards and Therapeutic Potentials. Council on Scientific Affairs. JAMA 1981; 246:1823-7.

Maugh TH. Marijuana (II): Does it damage the brain? Science 1974; 185:775-6.

Maykut MO, ed. Health Consequences of Acute and Chronic Marijuana Use. Oxford: Pergamon Press, 1984: 7-11, 61, 241.

Nahas GG, comp. Toxicology and Pharmacology of Cannabis Sativa with reference to delta 9-THC. Bulletin on Narcotics 1972:24.

NIDA (National Institute on Drug Abuse, National Institutes of Health) INFOFAX. Marijuana 13551. http://www.drugabuse.gov/

Ralnick MA et al. Marijuana. In: Clinical Management of Drug Overdose. Haddad LM and Winchester JF, eds. Toronto: WB Saunders Co., 1983:434-43.

Vincent BJ et al. Review of cannabinoids and their antiemetic effectiveness. Drugs 1983; 25:52-62.

PARTY DRUGS:

Club Drugs 13674.National Institute on Drug Abuse, National Institute of Health. NIDA INFAX.

http://www.nida.nih.gov/Infofax/clubdrugs.html

Feds classify ketamine as controlled substance. Alcoholism and Drug Abuse Weekly. 1999;11:7 (August 2, 1999).

Galloway GP et al. Gamma-hydroxybutyrate: An emerging drug of abuse that causes physical dependence. Addiction 1997;92(1):89-96.

Gantt P et al. Gamma-hydroxybutyrate: An emerging drug of abuse that causes physical dependence. Addiction 1997;92(1):89

Leshner AI. A Club Drug Alert. NIDA Notes (National Institute on Drug Abuse) 2000; 14(6):3-5

Munroe J. 'Roofies': horror drug of the '90's. Current Health 2. 1997;24(1).

Seligman J and King P. 'Roofies": the date rate drug: this illegal sedative is plentiful – and powerful. Newsweek 1996:127 (February 26).

Stell IM and Ryan JM. (gamma)-Hydroxybutyrate is a new recreational drug that may lead to loss of consciousness. BMJ 1996;313:424.

Thomas G et al. Comma induced by abuse of gamma-hydroxybutyrate (GHB or liquid ecstasy):a case report. Brit Med J 1997;314(7073):35-6.

SOLVENTS:

Baerg RD et al. Centrilobular hepatic necrosis and acute renal failure in 'solvent sniffers'. Ann Intern Med 1970; 73:713-20.

Bass M. Sudden sniffing death. J Am Med Assoc 1970; 212:2075-79.

Block SH. The grocery store high. Am J Psychiatry 1978; 135:126-7.

Brilliant L. Nitrous oxide as a psychedelic drug. New Eng J Med 1970; 283:1522.

Brozovsky M et al. Glue sniffing in children and adolescents. NY State J Med 1965; 65:1984-89.

Cohen S. The hallucinogens and the inhalants. Psychiatr Clinics of N Am 1984; 7:681-8.

Comstock EF et al. Medical evaluation of inhalant abusers. In: Sharp CW, Drehm ML, eds. Review of inhalants: euphoria to dysfunction. Rockville: NIDA Research Monograph 15, 1977; 54.

Cox TC et al. Drugs and drug abuse: a reference text. Toronto: Alcoholism and Drug Addiction Research Foundation, 1983;74, 295.

Danto BL. A bag full of laughs. Am J Psychiatry 1978; 121:612-13.

Di Maio et al. Four deaths resulting from abuse of nitrous oxide. J Forensic Sci 1978; 23:169-72.

Fejer D et al. Changes in the patterns of drug use in two Canadian cities: Toronto and Halifax. Int J Addict 1972; 7:467-79.

Gruener N et al. Methemoglobinemia induced by transplacental passage of nitrites in rats. Bull Environ Contam Toxicol 1973; 9:44-8.

Haley TJ. Review of the physiological effects of amyl, butyl and isobutyl nitrites. Clin Toxicol 1980; 16:317-29.

Henry S. The lunch-hour drug and other legal highs. McLeans 1979, July 2:10-12.

Hindmarsh KW et al. Solvent and aerosol abuse. Can Pharm J 1980; 113:99-102.

Hindmarsh KW et al. Solvent abuse-attitudes and knowledge among Saskatchewan retailers. Int J Addict 1983; 18:139-42.

Jager M. Native gas-sniffing habit brings Ottawa onto scene. Toronto: Addiction Research Foundation. The Journal 1976; August 1:1.

Kamm RC. Fatal arrhythmia following deodorant inhalant. Forensic Sci 1975; 5:91-3.

Law NR et al. Gasoline – sniffing by an adult. J Am Med Assoc 1968; 204:144-6.

Linder RL et al. Solvent sniffing: a continuing problem among youth. J Drug Educ 1974; 4:469-73.

Litt IF et al. Danger...vapor harmful: Spot-remover sniffing. New Engl J Med 1969; 281:543-4.

Maickel RP et al. Acute toxicity of butyl nitrites and butyl alcohols. Res Commun Chem Pathol Pharmacol 1979; 26:75-83.

McFadden DP et al. Butyl nitrites – an example of hazardous noncontrolled recreational drugs. Res Commun Subst Abuse 1982; 3:233-36.

Oh SJ et al. Giant axonal swelling in 'huffer's' neuropathy. Arch Neurol 1976; 33:583-6.

Porter MR et al. Drug use in Anchorage, Alaska. J Am Med Assoc 1973; 223:657-64.

Powars D. Aplastic anemia secondary to glue sniffing. New Eng J Med 1965; 273:700-2.

Reinhardt CF et al. Epinephrine-induced cardiac arrhythmia potential of some common industrial solvents. J Occup Med 1973; 15:953-55.

Schmitt RC et al. Gasoline sniffing in children leading to severe burn injury. J Pediatr 1972; 80:1021-22.

Sigell LT et al. Popping and snorting of volatile nitrites: a current fad for getting high. Am J Psychiatr 1978; 135:1216-18.

Simmons RC. Accentuate the positive in drug education. Health Education. October 1980; 4-6.

Smart RG et al. Six years of cross-sectional surveys of student drug use in Toronto. Bull Narcotics 1975; 27:11-22.

Walter PV et al. Glue sniffing: the continuing menace. Drug Forum 1977; 5:193-97.

Wason S et al. Isobutyl nitrite toxicity by ingestion. Ann Intern Med 1980; 92:637-8.

Watson JM. Solvent abuse by children and young adults: a review. Br J Addiction 1980; 75:27-36.

Weston M et al. Youth health and lifestyles, a report of work in progress: Regina, Saskatchewan. Saskatchewan Health and University of Regina, 1980, p.43.

Wyse DG. Deliberate inhalation of volatile hydrocarbons: a review. Can Med Assoc J 1973; 108:71-4.

STEROIDS:

Bahrke MS et al. Psychological and behavorial effects of endogenous testosterone levels and anabolic-androgenic steroids among males. Sports Medicine 1990; 10 (5):303-337.

Brower KJ et al. Evidence for physical and psychological dependence on anabolic-androgenic steroids in eight weight lifters. Am J Psychiatry 1990; 147(4):510-512.

Brower KJ et al. Anabolic-androgenic steroid dependence. J Clin Psychiatry 1989; 50(1):31-33.

Conacher GN et al. Violent crime possibly associated with anabolic steroid use. Am J Psychiatry 1989; 146(5):679.

Derken G. Bureau of Voluntary Compliance Seminar. NABP 84th Annual Meeting, San Antonio, Texas. May 7, 1988.

Desgagne M. Anabolic steroids: Use and Abuse Profile in Canada. CPJ 1989;122(8):402-408.

Goldman B. Death in the locker room: steroids and sports. Iscarus Press, South Bend, Indiana. 1984.

Goldfien A. The gonadal hormones and inhibitors. In: Katzung B.G., ed. Basic and Clinical Pharmacology, 4th ed. Appelton and Lange, Connecticut. 1989; 493-516.

Hickson RC et al. Adverse effects of anabolic steroids. Med. Toxicol: Adverse Drug Exp. 1989; 4(4):254-271.

Hough DO. Anabolic steroids and ergogenic aids. AFP 1990; 41(4): 1157-1164.

Johnson MD et al. Anabolic steroid use by male adolescents. Pediatrics 1989; 83(6): 921-924.

Kashkin KB et al. Hooked on hormones? An anabolic steroid addiction hypothesis. JAMA 1989; 262(22): 3166-3170.

Lormimer DA et al. Cardiac dysfunction in athletes receiving anabolic steroids. DICP, The Annals of Pharmacotherapy 1990; 24:1060-1061.

McNutt RA et al. Acute myocardial infarct in a 22 year old world class weight lifter using anabolic steroids. American Journal of Cardiology 1988; 62:164.

Mottram DR. Anabolic steroids. In: Drugs in Sport. Human Kinetic Books. Campaign, Illinois. 1988;59-78.

Nuwer H. Steroids (a phamphlet). Franklin Watts, New York. 1990.

Pope HG Jr. et al. Affective and psychotic symptoms associated with anabolic steroid use. Am J Psychiatry 1988; 145(4): 487-490.

Schoepp G. The storm over anabolic steroids. Drug Merchandising May 1989: 28-32.

Science 1972; 176: 1399-1403.

Streator S et al. Anabolic steroid abuse and dependence. PharmAlert 1990;19(2).

Terney R et al. The use of anabolic steroids in high school students. AJDC 1990; 144:99-103.

Voy R. Illicit drugs and the athlete. American Pharmacy 1986; NS26(11):39-45.

TOBACCO:

Action on Smoking and Health (ASH). Chemicals in Cigarettes and Smoke. http://ash.org

Big Tobacco's Latest Double Talk. http://tobaccofreekids.org/report/doubletalk/

Centers for Disease Control and Prevention. Cigar Smoking Among Teenagers-United States, Massachusetts, and New York 1996. J Am Med Assoc 1997;278(1):17-19.

Gossel TA. The Physiological and Pharmacological Effects of Nicotine. US Pharmacist 1992;1-12.

Humble GC et al. Marriage to a smoker and lung cancer risk. Am J Pub Health 1987;77:598

NIDA Notes (National Institute on Drug Abuse). Teen Alternative to Cigarettes Has Higher Concentrations of Nicotine. 15 (1); 14 (2000).

Phoenix House, ACDE website (www.acde.org) Basic Facts About Drugs: Tobacco

Routh HB et al. Historical Aspects of Tobacco Use and Smoking. Clinics in Dermatology 1998;16:539-44.

Svendsen KH et al. Effects of passive smoking on the multiple risk factor intervention trial. Am J Epidemiol 1987;126:783

Targeting Tobacco Use, 1999: The Nation's Leading Cause of Death. (tobaccoinfo@cdc.gov).

U.S. Department of Health and Human Services, Public Health Service, Centers for Disease and Control and Prevention. Mobidity and Mortality Weekly Report. Volume 43 (RR-4). Preventing Tobacco Use Among Young People. A Report of the Surgeon General. March 11, 1994

Wynder EL. Tobacco Use – United States, 1900-1999. J Am Med Assoc 1999;282(23):2202-04.